Selling Online

Selling Online

Beyond eBay

Donny Lowy

iUniverse, Inc.
New York Lincoln Shanghai

Selling Online
Beyond eBay

All Rights Reserved © 2004 by Donny Lowy

iUniverse, Inc.

For information address:
iUniverse, Inc.
2021 Pine Lake Road, Suite 100
Lincoln, NE 68512
www.iuniverse.com

ISBN: 0-595-30958-5

Printed in the United States of America

Contents

Preface

This publication is designed to provide accurate and authoritative information in regard to the subject matter covered. It is sold with the understanding that the author is not engaged in rendering legal, accounting, financial, investment, or other professional service. If legal advice or other expert assistance is required, the services of a competent professional person should be sought. The information in this book is only for educational purposes and should never be used unless one has first personally consulted with a licensed professional. By reading this book you are acknowledging that you could lose 100% of any money that you might decide to spend. You may read this book for entertainment or educational purposes but you should not use the information without the specific instructions of a professional who knows your personal situation.

Introduction

Recently there has been a lot of negative publicity regarding many Internet companies that seemed very promising upon first launching their operations. It seemed as if they were the roaring wave of the future destined to expand the economy across a new horizon. Many of these Internet companies carried a magnitude promise, which at the end of the day they simply did not deliver. As a matter of fact, most Internet companies, and it would probably be safe to say that over 90% of those that were started in the Internet boom of the late 90's and the year 2000, went out of business. Not only did they go out of business but also the majority that did stay in business did not reach profitability for a few more years, if at all. Most Internet companies sustained themselves by relying on investor funds and by soliciting funding from additional investors. So now, the question that should be on your mind is whether the odds are against your starting an Internet business or taking your business online. Not only are the odds seemingly stacked against success, but historically speaking most Internet business do indeed fail. Why even launch one when statistically it seems destined for failure?

Well, let me tell you about the actual reality. In fact, most Internet businesses that are around today do make money. Most online businesses are actually profitable and generate sizeable revenues for the owners of those businesses. Then why is it that we hear so much negative publicity about Internet businesses that fail? The reason is that most Internet businesses that were started were actually founded by people who lacked the required experience in running a successful business. The money that they had to run the business was spent too quickly. The money was soon gone and there were no profits or revenues to sustain the amount of money they were spending on their business. The Internet businesses that are successful have attained success because they have had managers and business owners with prior experience. Even if they did not have that much business experience, they were willing to follow time tested and proven ideas about how to run a business. Running an Internet business is like running any other type of business. It is necessary to have a strong fundamental grasp of your goals, including how the business will make money. There clearly must be a budget for the business to track the expenses and revenues closely for determining what you can do continuously to decrease expenses while increasing revenues. The problem with many of the public Internet companies and even the Internet companies that were not public is that they were having such an easy time getting funding from investors that they did not plan for a rainy day. Since it was so easy to get investor, funding the money seemed to be free and it was therefore spent accordingly. I am sure that you are aware from your personal life that when you work for money, you hold on to it much more prudently than money that you may have received as a gift. Consider how much more careful you are when you are spending money and making purchases with your own credit card or writing a personal check or spending cash? Think of this in comparison to spending a gift certificate that someone else has given to you.

This same situation occurred with many Internet companies. They actually received a gift certificate from investors that did not cost them anything except for their time spent in formulating a business plan. The business plan was presented to investors and the money began literally dropping out of the skies for the online entrepreneurs. Some of the online entrepreneurs did have good solid business plans but the problem resulted from their spending an excessive amount of money above what they should have been spending.

In their minds, they decided that not only would they definitely be making money but also that their online businesses would become profitable in a very short period. The reality is that this is impossible. It takes time to develop a business and even if it makes money from the beginning, you still must keep an eye on the big expenses or otherwise your spending will soon spiral out of control leaving nothing. Many business do not actually fail due to the lack of a promising model or because they are not making money. They fail because the expenses are too high and they simply do not have the money to pay them, so they soon cease function, file bankruptcy or just close the doors. If many online businesses had curtailed their spending habits they would have been about to reach their revenue and profitability goals before running out of money.

This explains the reason they invested in advertising to increase their business even when they did not have revenues to back the amount of advertising in which they were investing. In order for a company to go public, it needs to have a certain amount of revenue. It does not necessarily need to have a certain amount of profit. It only has to show a certain amount of sales revenue to prove that it is a solid company or that there is at least a solid business plan and that the company is actually involved in business. Many online entrepreneurs wanted only to be able to show investors that the business was growing and that soon it would be able to go public. How did they do that? They actually bought their customers by selling merchandise below cost and offering free shipping, which gave their customers enormous incentive to buy from them. Therefore, revenues increased rapidly allowing them to show their investors sales month after month while in reality, losses mounted. The reasoning behind this was that in taking the companies public they could say "look at our revenues, we have revenues of $100 million dollars, $200 million dollars, $5 billion dollars, $10 billion dollars and it is just a matter of time when we will reach profitability."

Consider the sales investors; whether they were investors before the company went public or investors who were buying the stock when it was already trading on the market, they were hearing "Since we have high revenues and it is only a matter of time before we show profitability, think about the high potential profitability. If we have projected revenues of $100 million dollars and we expect a profitability of 50% on the goods that we are selling." Investors were receiving promises that they would soon be having a profit of $50 million per year. This looks great on paper, but since they were running their business miles at a loss, and the business miles did not allow their making money on the businesses, there was no hope that profitability would ever be realized. This brings us back to square one, which is the first question. Why should you start an online business and why should you take your current business online?

Let me start out by saying that I strongly believe that regardless of what type of business you have, you can only benefit by taking your business online or by starting an online operation. Whether the reason you are considering an online business is to increase present revenues, have a higher profitability ratio, attract new customers, develop sales leads, gain new vendors, gain new suppliers or form deals that will only help your business grow, we will cover all your reasons in this book. In exploring these reasons step-by-step, you will see just how much your business can benefit from being online.

Having said this, I will tell you why taking your business online or why starting an online business is definitely a wise move for you and how you can avoid the mistakes made by other online entrepreneurs.

Your First Step: When you do start your online business, make sure that you first have in place a proven business plan that has been reviewed by a professional who clearly understands your business and has experience doing business online. You can find two consultants to work together—one who has experience in your industry and another who has experience in online business.

When you have the business plan, you next move will be in testing it. Instead of fully launching the business and starting to spend large sums of money, you will learn in this book how to develop a system that will allow you to measure your advertising results, the amount you should be spending on your advertising, and your true profitability per customer. We have a system that allows you to determine these factors ahead of time, meaning that it allows you to develop those factors before you actually start your online business or before you apply all your resources into the business. You will be able to gauge if your business has a future, if your business is heading in the right direction and if your business can actually make money online.

I believe that most businesses can make online. If you discover that your business is not making money online then you need to review the factors that we have discussed and the factors that you will learn using the system that this book will give you. You will learn to adjust different areas of your business model to insure that your business is able to produce revenues that are above your business expenses and that your business is headed toward profitability.

You will see that starting an online business can actually work for you and can be extremely lucrative as long as you have a clearly defined step-by-step business plan that is tested and which shows on a gradual basis that your business can make money and that it indeed will make money. As there are no guarantees in business, there is likewise no guarantee that by using this book you will make money. There is no guarantee that you will either lose money or make money. What I can guarantee is that if you will closely study the book applying its techniques and strategies, tips and methods as suggested in the text you will have a very good opportunity of not only having a profitable online business but also having an online business that can make you wealthy.

I am not promising any "get rich success stories" but rather that if you are willing to put in the work and the time, you will be able to develop a promising online business. I know of many online entrepreneurs who make anywhere from an extra $300.00 to $500.00 per week running their online business. I also know of online entrepreneurs who are making up to $20k per month or more with an online business. So as you can see, having an online business can help you make money whether you are selling packaged foods, collectibles, clothing, electronics, music or services. Whatever area you decide to focus on or whatever business you are currently involved in can only benefit by going online as long as you carefully follow a step-by-step business plan that is tested and proven.

Remember, doing business online is actually very similar to doing business offline. There are no differences as far as the nature of people, the needs, wants and benefits for which people are looking. The difference lies in the marketing approach, service approach, advertising approach and delivery approach that you implement in an online business.

Step Two: Your next step is to start thinking about what kind of online business you want to start or making the decision to take your current business online. You might want to make this decision when you are finished reading this book or even right now. Either way, as you read this book, I strongly suggest that you take notes, mental or hard copy, tracking how the ideas and strategies or methods suggested in the text can be applied to your business venture. One interesting thing happening whenever people read a motivational or business book is their becoming motivated and excited and having their imaginations start working. We know that when a person's imagination starts working they come up with new ideas and new approaches that they did not have before being motivated. You will want to keep a notebook handy while you read this book for ideas that pop into your mind so that you will be ready to put the ideas to work and apply those ideas to your business. If you forget your idea later, you will have a record of it.

Many of the ideas that I have had in business and many of the methods that I come up with were inspired while I was either reading a business book, listening to a business speaker, having a discussion with a fellow entrepreneur or fellow business author. You see, many of the ideas that we have, many of the methods that we produce, and many of the business virtues that we are able to use are not strictly originated from books or teachers but rather actually emanated from our own minds after having been guided in the right direction by reading a business book or by discussing our plans with a fellow online entrepreneur, a fellow business entrepreneur or someone else in whom we trust and confide.

Now you are ready to read this book and benefit from it. The most vital aspect in reading this book is in keeping an open mind and to remembering to be positive. You will need to be able to push out all of the negative ideas regarding Internet businesses. I can assure you that if you are not able to push the negativity from your mind you are not going to enjoy the benefit of actually grasping and applying the ideas successfully. If you are positive, and I know that you are since you picked up this book and are reading it, which clearly demonstrates your willingness to learn and to venture for growth in business and to explore new opportunities, this book is tailor-made for you. I believe that you will productively benefit from it and now invite you to read Chapter One.

Chapter One

When deciding upon an online business venture to start, or upon deciding how to run an online business, one of the most important concepts that you will have to grasp and remember is that success depends largely on your familiarity and your educational level regarding the industry or area in which you will be doing business. In order for you to have a good opportunity and to have a reasonable chance of being successful in your online business, you will have to operate in a familiar area. The reason is that the more familiar that you are with a given industry, the better the changes that you will be familiar with the needs of your customers and the benefits for which those customers are looking. Running an online business is like running an offline business, which is actually similar to any hobby or any activity that you are involved with in your daily life. The better that you understand the activity and the more that you know about it, the better you will be able to perform that activity. Not only is this true, but the more that you are interested in an activity, the more motivated you will be in your efforts and you will be able to improve the results of that activity. If you want a successful online business, you need to be involved with an online business with which you are familiar. You have to be involved in an area in which you are clearly interested. Many online entrepreneurs did not achieve the success that was possible simply because they were trying only to make money, which is not an unrealistic goal, but they should have also been operating their business in an area in which they were interested. They would have been very excited and very motivated and would have applied more energy. Also, if they had been intimately involved with the industry in which they operated in before they started their online business, they would have understood a lot more about the business process. They would have understood what it takes to sell to a customer, how to properly market to a customer, how to properly get a customer interested in buying or selling the merchandise or services which they were offering. They would have known how to find customers, the best suppliers of their products and services, and the best brands of products and services to offer. When running an online business, in

1

effect you are putting yourself in the position of the customer and asking yourself "What is the best way for someone to reach me? What is the best way for someone to sell to me? What is the best way for someone to convince me to buy his or her product or service? How would I like to buy their product or service?" If you are not excited about the product or service with which you are involved, you are not going to consider all the steps you should consider. You will not be taking any concrete steps to understanding the customers, what they want to purchase or the best means of contacting them. If you are not interested, then you will simply lose your grasp, as it is an arduous process, especially at the beginning when you are developing your online business. Therefore, I strongly recommend and you will find for yourself that most other savvy business people will also recommend, that you only involve yourself in a business that meets two criteria: No. 1—It must excite you to the point that you are involved in and enjoy the business so that you will look forward to spending time and energy on it. You will enjoy it so much that you will imagine more opportunities on your own because you will receive more satisfaction. You will have to be familiar with the business in which you are involved. No. 2—It must be a business that you must understand regarding the types of products and services that customers within your scope will buy, their intended use of those products and services, and the true benefit that they desire to receive from those products and services

Many people start businesses that are offshoots of their personal hobbies for the reason that it allows them to be involved in an area in which they are already experienced and enjoy. This makes them uniquely qualified to understand what their customers are attracted to and what their customers are willing to buy or sell.

I know of a successful online business operator who sells comic books. His comic book business generates hundreds of thousands of dollars per year in profit simply because it is a business that with which he is intimately familiar, in which he is very experienced; so therefore he understands how to market to comic book readers and collectors, how to reach his target customers and for what they are looking. He knows where all of the sources are located, how to buy the comic books, where to obtain the best prices, and how to sell the products at the best price level allowing him to make money while at the same time giving his customers a good value for their money.

I also know of online entrepreneurs who sell chocolate online. The reason that they sell chocolate is that at a basic level they like and enjoy chocolate themselves. They know that they are selling the products in the chocolate market because they have tested the chocolate themselves and enjoy it. They are familiar with how to market chocolate, what people look for in chocolate, what need and benefit people seek to fulfill by purchasing chocolate online, what types of chocolates are best when given as gifts, what types are best served with dinner and what types are best eaten as a snack. Since they are intimately familiar with the chocolate industry from being chocolate consumers themselves who are excited about the product, they are able to develop a very successful online chocolate business.

Make sure that the business you are starting online or the current business you want to take online is a business about which you are excited. If you are already running a successful business that does not honestly, interest you very much I would not recommend your taking that business online unless you have another individual who is going to be specifically devoted to running the online business. There are specific challenges with which you might not want to deal once you encounter them if you are genuinely not interested in the business that you are running.

Many people fall into a business, inherit a business, are a partner in a business or have just started a business in which they have lost all interest. These people continue to run the business because they need to make money to cover their bills and they enjoy the profits that the business produces. If however, they are not excited about the business, they are going to have very hard time starting a second business that deals with the same market as the current business in which they are not interested. This would be similar to someone not enjoying reading a French book but deciding to continue reading the French book, through a feeling of obligation for either intellectual reasons or professional reasons, but also deciding that he is going to start listening to French music. You can be sure that this person will soon give up listening to the French music which takes a more advanced skill than simply reading a French book which he will soon also stop reading. This is the same as a person running any business that they really do not enjoy. If they were to start an online business in the same industry or based on the same area that they do not enjoy, they could end up abandoning both businesses.

If you have a current business that you are running or have a full time occupation that you really do not enjoy, this does not mean that you cannot start on online business. What it does mean is that if you decide to start an online business, you can determine your hobbies, what area of running a business you would enjoy, and then start an online business specifically in this area. This is a great way to supplement your income or develop a full time income that could offer you a higher earning level than your present job or present business.

Many people who start an online business do it because they have difficulties at their work and they see issues that are not being addressed at work and realize that if they start an online business they could cater to the issues and solve the dilemmas faced in their corporate job or service job while running their own business. Online and offline entrepreneurs have started businesses when their vendors and suppliers were not delivering on time or were not delivering good products or did not deliver good service. This motivated them to start online businesses that catered to people running the same type of businesses that they themselves started.

For instance, if someone had a book store and it was very time-consuming to order books from a specific distributor due to disorganization, time lag in cataloging their books and in shipment of orders processed because everything was done manually by telephone, the owner of the bookstore could go online and start an online business wholesaling books to fellow bookstore owners. Since he already knows the problems and challenges that bookstore owners faced, he could solve the dilemmas by offering the bookstore owners an automated service through which bookstore owners could order their books online. The web site could deliver an order slip to someone who would actually pack up the books and ship them out the same day via UPS, FedEx or U.S. Mail.

The point of this example situation is that many times you can start an online business by identifying a certain need that is not currently being met to satisfaction whether it is at the corporate level, the consumer level or even the personal level. Many matchmaking sites are specifically set up because people have a hard time finding dates and these websites serve the need of bringing people together who otherwise may not meet. They offer connections between people who might be in different social circles but still would enjoy meeting each other. These sites also help people to screen their potential dates prior to actually meeting the person. Contact is facilitated through e-mail, telephone conversations, reading about each other's interests via their profiles, and actually viewing pictures of each other. Afterwards they can decide if they are actually attracted to one another and determine if they want to meet and go out together. Since looks is not everything, they have the opportunity to have conversations, read about the other person and continue benign contact until they are comfortable enough to meet. Matchmaking sites on the Internet produce millions of dollars in profits because they are fulfilling a personal need that can be tremendously felt and experienced by every single person not only in the United States, but also in every country around the world. Every person wants to find a match. Every person wants someone with whom he or she can share his or her dreams and their lives. The online matchmaking sites allow this by bringing people together and also offering a certain amount of security and protection as opposed to being set up or meeting a complete stranger.

When you start your online business, make sure that it is based on a need that you personally have or that your relatives, friends or business associates all have in common. This will provide you the means for investigating the possibilities further. You will be able to ask people for what they are looking and what will make them comfortable. You will be able to decide whether people would use this type of product or service. This way you will know if your business idea is a potentially successful idea not just offline but online as well. If the answer is "no" you can ask people what you can do to meet the need and insure that they will use your service. Many websites use focus groups to come up with the answer. A focus group is people organized by private business. The groups come together and are asked many questions to determining what type of products they like, what type of services they like, what price is considered a fair price, what price is considered an expensive price, what quality for which they are looking and what brands they prefer. Focus groups can cost up to $50k for a one-hour session. Think how much money you could gain by creating your own focus group.

How is a focus group established? You pick an area of business in which you know people use your product or service or you yourself use that product or service and present your questions to them. By their collective responses, you will clearly know if you are on the right track and if you are delivering a product or service that people will want to use. If it is something with which you are very familiar you will always know how to adjust your product or service and your marketing and advertising efforts from knowing what people truly prefer and enjoy regarding the need or desire that your product or service fulfills.

Chapter Two

Here we will discuss the need for conducting extensive research and determining the correct type and amount research required to run a successful online business. As mentioned in the previous chapter, the familiarity within an area is extremely important when running an online business. You need a tremendous amount of research to determine if your product or service will be successful. The right amount and type of research has to be based on someone or an organization that has a personal involvement with the market in which you will be dealing. Whoever provides your research will have to be unbiased. In many situations the people or entities that you will get your information from are, by the very nature of what they are or what they represent, biased or influenced to some degree. It is important to keep this in mind. To one extent, you want to have as much unbiased information as possible. However, the nature of life is that many of the areas from which you need to get information by their very nature are biased, but you will still need to get information from them. You will have to keep in mind their vested stake in the information and their desires as far as the outcome of your decision. For example, if you approached a law school and asked, "Is it possible to have a promising career today as a lawyer?" the law school of course would respond, "Yes, it is possible." This does not mean that you cannot have a promising career as a lawyer, since most lawyers do have good successful careers. It also means that the law school to wants you to enroll in its curriculum because that is their business…they have students who pay tuition to cover their salaries and to bring in revenues for the law school. This does not mean that the advice is rogue or inaccurate, but it is important to remember why they are giving you this advice and what they have at stake in your decision.

Many times when you receive information from a source that is unbiased and that has nothing at stake in your decision, the advice that you get may not be solid because the person or the organization rendering this advice really has no involvement with you, the business in which you are involved or with your pursuits. Therefore, they might not care as much as an organization or individual who is involved with the area of business in which you are concerned. In these types of situations, the best thing to do is have a balanced level of information. You will want to have sources of information from people who are intimately involved with the area in which you want to operate. You want to have people who use your product or service that you wish to sell online. You want to have advice from other people who run their businesses online. At the same time, you want to have advice from people who are familiar with the business, online or offline, and advice from people who understand what you want to do.

You also want to have advice from people that you simply trust. It is very important not to take advice from negative people. The reason is not that their advice is not good, but that people who are negative will always have a negative attitude towards anything they discuss. They will put a negative spin on anything that arises. Some of these people are not very happy or successful with the experiences of their daily lives. Some do not feel that they could succeed in what you want to try to accomplish. On the inside, many of these people want the opportunity to start their own business, but due to social pressures, family pressures or personal situations they cannot start a business. On the other hand, if you get advice from positive people only, you may be misled by thinking that they will only tell you what you want to hear. This is not accurate. Positive people will still give good advice but will also go on to tell you when an idea does not work. At the same time, they will not start out predisposed towards discouraging you. Contrary to discouraging you, positive people will always look for a way to help you make things happen. Even if your business plan does not seem to be an accurate formula for online success, genuinely positive people will work with you to try to help develop your business plan further and adapt it to the online business world so that you will be able to succeed online.

The people with whom you should be discussing your business plan you are family members with whom you are close, trust and respect. Seek advice from select family members whose past business advice has been proven reliable, friends who know your strengths as well as your weaknesses, and business associates who will not see you as competition and who have thing to lose if you start an online business. Business associates who have something to gain by you starting an online business can be helpful even though they will only push you to start your online business because of their gain. These people will want you to start your online business simply because if they have something to gain, it also means that they have something to gain by your success. Therefore, not only will they give you good advice but also they will help you with good connections in starting and developing the business, and from there to continuing support that will help you prosper. They are keenly aware that your gain is their gain as well.

Who else can you go to for information regarding your online business? Trained groups focused on the area with which you will be dealing provide valuable information. Consult industry groups such as The Chocolate Manufacturers Association of America if you are planning to sell chocolates online. You could ask them for advice as far as your idea and whether they feel that it could do well online. Another question could be regarding the specific types of chocolates that you want to market. What areas of the country enjoy this type of a chocolate? What areas of the country are looking for different types of chocolates? What products are seasonal in nature? What products sell all year long?

These questions are true for any type of association that you contact for any type of product or service that you offer. Usually the industry associations will be able to give you free advice that ordinarily would cost you thousands of dollars from a consultant. The advice will be given to you free because the association wants its industry to grow, it wants you buy from industry members, and it actually wants your membership in the association.

You must be careful not to reveal your entire business plan because you do not want them to pass on information inadvertently to another member who can then use your idea and beat you to the draw. When approaching these trade associations keep the actual important day-to-day details of your business to yourself but discuss with the them the general idea of your business and ask them about the best ways to market your product or service online, the best products and services to market online within this industry, and the needs had by consumers in this industry, as well as the benefits for which the consumers are looking.

As you notice, I keep mentioning benefits and needs separately because they are two clearly distinct concepts that we will discuss later. I will explain the differences between the concepts and your need to insure that you are covering both of the concepts in order for you to be successful in running an online business.

Another strategy for gaining good advice is by reading trade journals that cover an industry. You can pick up these journals at a business library and familiarize yourself with the events that are taking place in the industry, the products and services that are doing well, the products and services that are not in demand, customer expectations for receipt of the products or services, prices that are being paid, the current industry needs, the current benefits, the current issues facing the industry, and the specific current issues that need to be addressed. Reading a trade journal will give you an accurate and deep insight into the real core issues that are being dealt with in the business. I can almost guarantee that by reading the trade journals that cover your industry you will be able to gain advice ranging from how to start your online business, where to take your business online, how to reach your customers effectively or how to sell to your customers the effectively. Even though these details will not be spelled out, you will actually be told how to start an online business and how to market your online business. When all of these issues are glaring you in the face, you will clearly know how to develop your online business using the strategies and constants discussed in this book. You will understand how to tailor a solution for handling the issue and making that solution produce positive results using the information regarding those issues published in the trade journal.

Likewise, you can contact people involved in your industry. As long as they do not feel that you are competition to them, they are usually happy to help you. In most industries, the market is so large that even if you are a new player and might become a competitor they will not feel threatened especially if they already have an established business. They will probably be happy to discuss the business with you since people usually enjoy talking and discussing their work. They know that by their giving advice that you may be able to do the same thing for them on an equal basis as your business grows. In order to gain information from people you can also offer to give them advice such as how to run an online business by reminding them that the online market is large enough for various businesses. Since the market is so large, you can do this effectively as long as you do not give any of your trade secrets. You do not want to actually create competition, but to make gain in your own market you can test out ideas on this fellow business owner.

Networking is also very important. You should actively develop a list of contacts in the industry you will be involved in so that you can always have someone to call to ask questions, follow up on ideas, to find suppliers and vendors through contacting them, to learn the new issues, how to stay current regarding the new products and services, and to develop contacts within the industry such as other people working online.

Everything that we have discussed regarding the industry is also true for developing contacts within the online world. People who are online marketers can share ideas and discuss trends. The same goes for web designers for learning the latest web design techniques, design developments, web site development, and marketing skills such as ways to make your own web site more exciting.

You should develop contacts with people who produce ad copy since this is especially important in the Internet world where the customer cannot normally speak to you but rather has to rely on information being given on the web site regarding their decision to purchase. Even if the customer does speak to you, their first reaction is still going to be formed by looking at your online web site or reading an e-mail, which are both examples of ad copy. Developing a contact with people who write ad copy is helpful so that they can tell you the best way to write ad copy. You can share all of your own ideas for ad copy, which will make them more willing to share ideas with you.

You will need contacts with people running online business even if they are unrelated to your own industry because their marketing concepts can still be helpful to running your own online business. People who do business online have many of the same challenges as people doing business offline, so quite naturally everybody benefits when strategies are developed with other online business entrepreneurs. The issues vary widely from marketing, payment issues, to delivery issues. Many of the delivery issues are the same regardless of what businesses are delivering to customers. It could be chocolates, books, electronics or any item that needs to be delivered correctly.

There are also various trade forums taking place online. You can look for web sites that have message boards where people post questions and comments regarding the industry in which they are operating. These forums also are devoted to people who run businesses online, some of which are general in nature where different issues are discussed such as marketing, advertising, or product and service pricing. Some forums are very specific to the industry to which they are related. I remember finding a message board for people who are operating second hand stores, stores that cater to people who want to purchase used goods and would rather save money than having to spend retail prices on new items. These customers would rather not spend a lot of money but they still want good quality items for a fraction of the cost.

There are many forums on line such as book sales, clothing sales, and e-bay business development sales. There are forums to help people make money while helping other people start their own online businesses. Regardless of what type of business that you want to start online there are forums that exist to help. Some online forums have nothing to do with online business. These are also great sources of information for you. There are gatherings from conventions, meetings, and lectures given by online entrepreneurs and lectures by industry entrepreneurs covering the business in which you want to be involved. Attend as many lectures as possible as long as the lectures are giving concrete information for your business development.

You want to attend these lectures to develop contacts for creating a network of people with whom you can make contact to discuss your business ideas. As you develop this network, you will also be exposed to opportunities. These opportunities will vary such as merchandise purchasing at low cost as well as selling your merchandise at better prices than you could in the past. However if you decide to develop your business you will always need people who are already doing business online and people who are involved in your own industry so that you can develop new approaches to all areas of your business. Going to trade groups and discussions regarding an online business or regarding your industry of focus is especially helpful from the marketing point of view because you will also be able to gain new customers by finding out who is looking for the products or services that you want to provide. You could actually meet people at the lecture who are great customers and may be buying from one of your competitors or might not even be buying from anyone and you can be the supplier of the product or service to that customer.

Running an online business involves networking, collecting information, where to find that information and how to objectively look at that information based on the source of the information. If you can develop a good system based on everything that we have discussed such as continually gathering and absorbing more information plus systematically studying the information that you receive, you will be able to develop a very strong business that will grow and overcome the challenges that most online businesses face.

Chapter Three

When starting your online business you need to keep in mind that the nature of the consumer is still the same as the consumer in relation to an offline business. This means that when you sell to your consumer, whether it is a product or a service; remember no matter what type of business you have, you are always selling. When you sell to that consumer, you need to determine the actual needs of that market place and the benefits for which that market place is looking. In other words, you need to know at 100% accuracy what the customer is looking for, what need they have that must be fulfilled, and what benefits they are seeking from providers of services or products in that marketplace. For instance if you go into a health food store that is selling vitamins, the customers in the store are not looking to purchase vitamins. A plastic capsule of powdered vitamins is useless to them. What the consumer wants in that situation is the nutrients that will help him feel better, become healthier, produce weight loss, strengthen his heart or build muscle so that he can enjoy a healthier lifestyle and live a longer life. There are many different benefits that the consumer desires to obtain from the product. His need is to get healthy, stay healthy and live longer.

The same principal applies to an online business. Before entering into a certain marketplace you have to determine the need for that market place and what benefits are desired in that marketplace. Amazon.com does a great job selling books online because they have determined their customers' needs the benefits their customers seek in buying books online. As far as the needs, Amazon.com realizes that people want to become informed, educated, experience growth in their lives and also be entertained by reading books. The need is to advance one's life through intellectual stimulation, developing a hobby, learning a skill, getting a better job or making more money with investments or personal business. Books provide entertainment as an alternative to watching a movie rental or taking a walk in the park. Amazon.com has taken all of this into consideration and has formulated a concept to fulfill this need. It has set up an operation whereby people can visit its web site and view various categories and subcategories that makes it very easy for a person to find the books for which they are looking. The benefits are similar to the needs when they order books from Amazon.com Among the benefits is not having to go to a bookstore, not having to spend hours looking around for books by calling different bookstores to see whether they have certain books. Its customers also save money along with their time. Since Amazon.com is very careful to determine their consumers' needs and benefits, it has a very successful business.

Barnes & Noble.com has been able to do the same thing but it differentiates itself from Amazon.com by allowing its customers to pick up orders at its stores. Amazon.com does not allow customers to pick up an order at a store thereby allowing its customers to save on shipping, but it still sells more books than Barnes & Noble sells. This is the result of Amazon.com simply being keenly aware a customer need that Barnes & Noble ignored, which is the need customers have to order a book online because they specifically do not want to have to go to a bookstore and stand in line or take time from their busy lives to go to a store and wait in line while a salesperson locates a book. Amazon.com is not very concerned with the fact that Barnes & Noble allows its customers to pick up the books at the store. Another thing that Amazon.com does just to make sure that it is not threatened by this pick up tactic is by offering free shipping on orders that are over a certain dollar amount. This means that a customer is required to order at least $25.00 in books and sometimes the minimum is raised to $50.00; however, most customers tend to purchase 2-3 books at a time so meeting the minimum is not a problem. Both of these companies also realize that one of the needs that they are fulfilling is that people like to buy books as gifts for someone else. That is not even the actual need...the actual need is that people want to develop good relationships with family members, friends and business associates which can be accomplished by giving these people gifts. Since they have set up their business model in such a way as to allow customers to buy gifts for other people they are able to fulfill this need. The benefits to the customers are that they do not have to go to a store, they are offered a large selection from which to choose, they can easily find the right gift for a specific individual and specific purpose and/or occasion, and they can have it delivered in a timely manner.

A feedback system is another great concept that both of these companies use to their benefit. The feedback system should be used in all online endeavors. This system is one that allows the customers to write reviews on the products and services that you offer. These two book companies allow customers to write reviews on different books that they have read. These reviews encourage customers to buy certain books by opening their minds to certain books that they might not have considered otherwise. If they see positive reviews, they are inclined to purchase the books. From time to time, there are negative reviews but there are usually positive reviews right next to the negative. Usually the people that you hear from the most are the people who complain, while you usually those you hear the least from are people who are happy because they are content and settled. These two book companies do not mind allowing negative feedback comments because they want to show the customer who sees positive feedback, that it is a genuine feedback from a reader. If customers only see positive feedback, they would be very skeptical and would say, "It doesn't make sense that everybody likes the book." By offering feedback on their websites both companies fulfill the needs of people who want make sure that they are buying the right thing. The benefit of them knowing that information is that they know they will be buying something that is actually going to help them because the feedback is positive, letting them know that it will help them. If you want to succeed, be sure that you have a feedback system for your products and services that allows customers to leave their experiences on your web site.

If you find that you are getting a lot of negative feedback then you know that your business strategy needs to be changed. You will need to modify the product or service and make sure that your customers are content. Even if you decide to ignore the negative feedback and you do not allow it to be posted, the fact that you are receiving a lot of negative feedback should send you a message. If you do not notice that message, you will eventually lose a lot of business because customers will go elsewhere to purchase their products and services. On the other hand, when customers see positive feedback they will be more encouraged to make a purchase. Therefore, it would be good to follow the example of the two book companies of having a system where customers can read what other customers' experiences were regarding your customer service, pricing and level of quality of products.

Let's go back to the discussion of understanding the true needs and benefits of the market in which you are considering going into business. Have you ever heard the expression "You don't sell the steak, but you sell the sizzle"? What that means is that a steak, which is a great tasting piece of beef, is not the thing for which people are looking. Consumers want the taste of meat and they want the satisfaction that comes from eating a well-cooked steak. My father happens to love steak and when he purchases it, he does not simply put it in the oven to cook it and eat it because he is not looking specifically just for the nourishment of the meat. He is looking for the satisfaction of enjoying a well-cooked steak. Actually, the want or need that is being fulfilled is the need to eat a good meal that you enjoy, feel good about and makes you happy. The benefit is that you are able to have that good meal as well as enjoy yourself and that you are able to enjoy something that you may not eat on an everyday basis. When you sell a product or service online ask yourself "What are people really looking for when it comes to the product or service that you are offering? What is their need and what is the benefit for which they are looking to receive?" The reason that this is very important is because once you understand the true needs and benefits you will know how to market your products and services correctly. If you do not know how to market your products or services correctly, you will end up marketing, advertising and promoting components of your products or benefits of your products or services for which people are not really looking.

For example, if a car manufacturer wants to sell cars online and it advertises that if consumers buy from them they will throw in a brand new CD player, then this is a benefit that people may enjoy. However, those customers may still say to themselves "You know I'm really not too sure if I specifically need that CD player." This is not fulfilling a need because it is only being advertised as an added feature to the car and customers know that they could go to a local dealer that sells in person and negotiate different features including a CD player. On the other hand, if the car manufacturer that wants to sell cars online would take a step back and ask itself "What are the true needs that customers need fulfilled?" they may say to themselves that one of the needs my customers really needs fulfilled is the need to have a high quality car and we will provide benefits according to what the customer designates. So how you can do this? You could offer cars online that are tailor made to the customer's interest level. You would advertise through the web site that customers could order cars with the exact accessories and features that they need personally. When a customer sees an advertisement like this it they will recognize it as fulfilling their needs because they will say to themselves, "Whatever I need in a car, I can obtain by ordering my car from this web site as opposed to going to a dealer where the car that I want may not be in stock and if it is in stock, it may not have all the features and accessories for which I am looking."

Another need that people have is to have an easier life. They do not want to haggle, argue or fight. If this car manufacturer sets up a web site and advertises that the vehicles are factory direct, below wholesale with the lowest possible prices available, and advertised that in ordering from this web site people will not have to negotiate as the prices are already the lowest, it will fulfill the need of people who do not like to haggle and want an easy shopping experience. The benefit that those people will receive is having a car that is priced fairly without having to negotiate that fair price. The benefits that you are offering can be the same ones as you would ordinarily offer for a product or service. What you have done differently is to ask yourself what are the needs that consumers want to have fulfilled and what benefits do they want.

Let me now stress how the product or service will fulfill those needs and give them those benefits. An example is a hammer. Nobody needs a hammer and nobody needs a nail. I am sure, however, that it is not possible to have any construction in this world without having a hammer and nails. We do see that millions and millions of hammers and nails are purchased every year. On the other hand, I am telling you that I am sure after I explain this to you that nobody really wants a hammer and nobody really wants a nail.

A hammer is a piece of metal that is shaped in a specific way for performing a certain function, which is to knock nails into a wall, knock nails into a piece of wood or pull out those nails. The nails are used to hang up pictures, to lock a piece of hardware into place, to put a door into a house, to remodel or to construct or many other things. However, nobody per se wants a hammer or nails. What they want is to have the remodeled house. They want the house to have a door in the doorway. They want to hang a picture on the wall. These are their needs. The needs are to have a house that looks nice. Their need is to be able to finish a construction project. Their need is to build something. The benefit is having a nice house. The benefits in total come from having a finished product, a remodeled bath or kitchen or the compensation that they will receive for doing construction work for someone else. The money is a benefit that they will receive from doing their work.

However, if somebody came to the people who are involved in construction and said "Here is a magic lamp from which when rubbed, a Genie will appear. You can request from the Genie that you be allowed to do any construction work that you choose." In this case, any sane individual would opt for the Genie simply because it would save a lot of time and work since the Genie could do the work. There are people who enjoy doing construction work as a hobby. The need of those people is actually doing something with their hands, which is fulfilling to them and the benefit is the fulfillment that they receive from taking pride in the work and from the actual action of the construction. In that situation, if someone introduced not a hammer but a different tool that did the job even better or allowed him or her to really feel like they were doing construction work; they would opt for the other tool.

When you market a hammer online or you market nails online you have to realize the need that is being fulfilled and the benefits to the people who are looking for the products. The way that I would market a hammer and nails online would be with a web site that stressed how these are the perfect hammers to for using in perfect home remodeling jobs. "These nails will keep your frames on the walls for a minimum of 5 years. These nails are guaranteed to keep doors from falling off the frame for a minimum of 10 years." You see, I am actually stressing the need people have and the benefits for which they are looking. These needs must be fulfilled and the benefits must be received. I could further stress the fact that this hammer is the most comfortable hammer that can be used, that it has the most strength, and that by using this hammer you do not have to use a lot of effort to drive the nail. When advertising the nails I would let people know that the nails go through the material extremely easily and could penetrate any piece of wood or wall with ease. This is stressing the benefit as well as the need to be fulfilled so that they can enjoy their work or their hobby without having to over exert themselves.

If you are advertising a leather jacket online, which is a great product because it is high-end item that people may not have in the local area where they live and they could purchase it for themselves or for someone else as a gift. Since it is a high-end item, it would give you plenty of a profit margin. Remember, when someone buys a leather jacket, the need is not the same as buying a regular jacket because if one is simply cold, he does not have to buy a $200.00 leather jacket but could rather go to a local department store and purchase a $40.00 or $50.00 heavy winter jacket that will keep him warm. As a matter of fact, a leather jacket really will not keep you that warm, especially compared to a winter jacket or any other type of jacket. You could say that the need of wearing a leather jacket is for a person to look nicer; however, that is not really the need issue because there are other ways for a person to look nice. For instance, one could dress with a nice shirt, good pants or quality shoes. So what is the true need that they are trying to fulfill? The true need is that they want to not only dress nicely but that they want to feel better about themselves by wearing a high fashion item and give the appearance to other people that they are fashionable. The actual need is that they want to be socially accepted and to fit in with other people by making a good impression with people because they want people to look up to them. This is a true need that some people have in wearing a leather jacket…making a really good impression on other people so they can either be socially accepted or so that they will be admired and looked up to by others.

Therefore, when you advertise your leather jacket you would want to stress how nice people will look wearing this jacket and the reaction of other people when someone is seen wearing the jacket. You would want testimonials from people who say that when wearing the leather jacket they have attracted the attention of other people and have received many compliments. You would want to stress in your ad copy how the leather jacket has the look of a $2,000.00 jacket. Remember, it is image that is very important, the need for people to look very good and upscale. At the same time, the benefit is being able to fit in with people, feeling good about oneself, getting compliments on the jacket and showing the jacket off in public. You would want to stress in your ad copy and your web site that by wearing this leather jack, the buyer will receive all of the benefits for which they are looking. You do not want to take up space on your web site stressing what type of leather went into the manufacturing of the jacket. People do not usually care what type of leather is used as long as they know that it is high quality leather. In fact, if you look carefully at catalogs or websites that sell leather jackets, when they describe the leather that is being used, it is described in a way that tells people that others will be very impressed when they see them wearing the leather jacket. They do not simply tell people, "We use lambskin." but rather they tell people that when their friends see them wearing a lambskin jacket they will be extremely impressed because people know that lambskin jackets are expensive. The same is true in this situation. When you stress the benefits of wearing the leather jacket, remember what it is for which people are looking. They do not want to know that it is manufactured in Italy, in the United States or France. What they want to know is that the reason it is such a big deal that the jacket is manufactured in Italy is because when people see someone wearing Italian leather jackets, they are so impressed by those jackets that they assume the person wearing it must be a shrewdly good dresser, an affluent person and a very impressive individual. You want to stress all of those components of the jacket. You can let people know who manufactured the jacket but let them know who manufactured it in a way that will excite them to wear the jacket by once again stressing how their needs will be fulfilled and what benefits they will receive by wearing the jacket.

If you have a web site devoted to selling candies, remember that people do not buy candy because they are hungry. If people are hungry, they can walk into any supermarket and buy food. If they are going to buy candy from your web site, they are also not looking for candy that will give them instant gratification. If they simply want a chocolate bar or a bag of M & M's or chewing gum, they could walk into the local store and purchase the items. If people are going to buy candy online you have to ask yourself, "What need is being fulfilled and what are the benefits for which they are looking?" I would say to myself that if someone is taking the step of looking for candy online when they can easily go to a local store to buy candy, then the reason they are going online is that they are looking for an experience that they cannot obtain at a local convenience store. Therefore, the candy will have to be portrayed as very exclusive candy that is unique and difficult to find and that there is a reason why they are very exclusive. You need to stress their exclusivity. You want to stress the reason why people would want to buy these candies and you want to show them how hard it is to find your product. You have then done two things...you have aroused their curiosity which means they will want to know more about the candies so they will order the product to try them. Upon trying your candies, they will see that the candy is indeed exclusive and unavailable anywhere else, so when the customer is in the mood for an exclusive type of candy, an expensive candy or a great tasting candy that is not found in a convenience store he will know that he found it on your web site. Therefore, you would have to stress all of these points, which are that your candies are...

No. 1: Exclusive candies that cannot be found at the local stores.

No. 2: Difficult to find candies, even at upscale candy stores.

No. 3: Incredibly delicious candies worth buying online and also worth spending more money for than candies offered at a convenience store.

The need that people have is to have something special and unique, which creates the reason for them to buy candy online. The benefit is being able to enjoy the great tasting candy, to impress their friends by sharing such an exclusive and hard to find candy and giving away the product to their friends, co-workers, relatives or business associates with the additional benefit of being able to impress the recipients of the gift. You will want to be able to express in your ad copy that the candies make such an excellent gift because anyone who receives them will be very impressed with the candies and will be extremely grateful to the person who gave it to them. You see it is very important in your ad copy to always realize that you are never actually selling a product or service but rather you are selling the benefits that the product or service delivers and you are fulfilling a need by delivering a product or service.

With all of this in mind, think of the area that you have decided to focus in and if you have not yet decided to focus in an area that is okay; however, you should start considering different areas. I suggest that you do the following mental exercise. Select the area that you are focusing in on or the area that you are considering focusing on. Write down on paper different products or services that are purchased in the area in which you are considering doing business. Proceed then to making a list of the true needs that people are looking to have fulfilled and the benefits the product or service delivers. Each time you identify a need, look at the need very closely and then again ask yourself "What is the true need?" Take it to the next level and the level after that until you see how deeply you can go. It would be the same way as if someone said to me, "What is the true need of a beverage?" The first thing that I would say is refreshment. I would take it further and say that people do not just want to be refreshed, but also to have refreshment that tastes great. Then I would surmise that this is not enough because there are plenty of drinks that taste great. It cannot be just that people want to just buy a great tasting drink so I might simply say that people are thirsty and want to quench their thirst. That need cannot be the right one because someone could drink water to have his or her thirst quenched. The next level would be that people want to be healthier so perhaps they need would be a healthy drink. Then I would ask again, "What is the true need behind wanting to be healthy?" After health, the next need would be that people want to be in good shape. This is not the true need. What is the true need beyond wanting to be in good shape? The true need would be that people want to impress other people by having a better physical appearance. Still, that is not the true need. Why would a person want to have an improved physical appearance, why would they want to be impressive to other people unless it is to have relationships with other people? As I go down the list, I come up with all of the true needs that this drink is fulfilling and then I market the drink according to those needs.

If you notice when you see beer or any liquor being advertised, especially online, they stress how the drinks will help people to become more socially accepted and that the drinks will help them develop relationships with the opposite sex. They emphasize that the drinks will help people develop good standing friendships and will help with business relationships. The people who market liquor and alcoholic beverages are aware that the true need is not to quench one's thirst, it is not to have a good tasting beverage, but it is to form relationships with other people and they demonstrate using the drink as a medium of forming those relationships. The need people have is relationships, so the drink is marketed as a tool for fulfilling this relationship need. So you can see that this is very different from the need that most people would assume that alcoholic beverages serve. Most people if asked about the need that these beverages fulfill would say that the need would be to relax, to be able to unwind or mellow out; however, that is not the real need. The true need in this case is for someone to be extremely relaxed, calm and comfortable and then you would have to market the drink as fulfilling these needs. If you say that the drink fulfills the needs of allowing relationship formation with other people, then you would market it accordingly. What you would not do is simply market the drink by stressing the taste, the caloric content or how the drink comes in a fashionable container since that is not what people want. You have to understand the true need.

Many breweries work specifically on this premise. Many places that serve drinks in their establishment know that people are coming to form relationships and therefore will set up the surroundings in a way that is conducive to socializing. Instead of just stressing which drinks they serve and heavily advertising the prices or the products, what they actually advertise is the ambience and the mood that is created and how their establishment allows people to meet and enjoy each other's company.

When starting your online business and developing your marketing strategy and your advertising copy, ask yourself what the true needs are for the people in your market and what the benefits are that they need to obtain. Then once you have a list of the needs and benefits, you can tailor your advertising and marketing strategies towards stressing how your product or service will fulfill those needs and deliver the benefits for which those people are looking.

Sometimes when you have a product or service that you are having a difficult time selling, you might have bought a product that was hot at one time but now the product is stagnant. You may have purchased a special closeout and now you are having a hard time selling the closeout. Instead of trying to sell that slow moving merchandise in the same market to which it is usually sold, think of what needs the product can fulfill and what benefits it can deliver to people. Then make a separate list of groups of people who could benefit from having that need fulfilled and who would want to receive those benefits. By matching up your lists, you will begin to succeed by having a good business strategy that will allow you to sell the product or service that you could not sell previously but which can now be sold to a different market altogether.

You can turn a slow moving product or service, which does not have much demand into a very fast hot selling product or service, which has a tremendous amount of demand in the right market. By doing this you will be able to stay ahead of the pack. You will distinguish yourself from most other business people who instead of stressing the need for fulfillment and the benefit deliverance, they end up stressing the actual qualities of their products or services. With your understanding of what you actually need to sell and what you actually need to market, you will be able to sell a lot more than your competition sells, therefore your increased sales will lead to increased profitability and will help your online business grow to new heights.

Chapter Four

In this chapter, we will discuss actually offering products or services that fulfill the needs of the market place that you are serving. We discussed in the previous chapter how to determine and how to discover the true needs of your market and what benefits consumers in that market are looking to obtain.

In this chapter, we will discuss actually offering products or services that will fulfill those needs. The first step is to make a list of the needs your market place is looking to have fulfilled and what benefits your market place is looking to obtain. Next, we need to make a list of products and services that help people fulfill those needs and help then obtain those benefits.

For instance, if you are serving a market place that is looking to lose weight, the weight loss market place that constitutes the majority of the United States and could constitute the majority of the world for that market, then your market place has the need of losing weight for various reasons. One reason could be social acceptance; another is to be more attractive, which actually is the need of using the formula we used before of always taking the need to the next step to discover the true need. In this situation, the true need is the need for someone to form a relationship with someone else and for social companionship. Another need is the desire to live longer, simply to feel better which actually means happiness. You would then look for products or services that would fulfill these needs. You might not want to sell treadmills because even though a treadmill seemingly does fulfill those needs and does provide the benefits your market place is looking for, it does not really match the needs of your market place. The actual need and the actual desire of people in the weight loss market place is to lose weight without having to put in much effort or time into the pursuit of weight loss. Therefore, a treadmill or any type of aerobic machinery or exercise machinery would actually not fulfill the need.

Weight loss pills on the other hand could fulfill that need, even though I do not recommend that anyone take them. I actually advise against taking them since I am not a doctor and do not profess to be a doctor. The reason I would not suggest these pills is that they can be extremely unsafe. Many of these pills have herbs in them that could be dangerous to consumers.

If someone did discover a weight loss pill that is extremely safe and helpful for people, then I would not have anything against people taking these pills. The reason why that I would rather market the weight loss pill instead of marketing the exercise machinery is because the pills fulfill the needs of someone being able to obtain a benefit without having to put forth much effort. The need that is being fulfilled is the need of having those desired results such as being socially accepted, being attractive, forming relationships with other people and not having to put forth much effort.

Another example is that if your market place is that of professional salespersons, the need that professional salespersons have is the need to find ways to increase their productivity and actually behind this is the need to make more money. The further need beyond this is the reason they would want the money, which is to have a better lifestyle, a nicer home and more for themselves and their families. Salespersons also want to spend less time doing their work and more time with their spouses, families and friends.

Therefore, I would market to this group of sales professionals software and any technology that allows them to work less and to have more results than what they would have otherwise without using the software technology. There is a software product that allows people to compile expensive databases containing all of their contacts. This software has become extremely successful among sales professionals because it allows them to save time by having a list of all the different people whom they encounter through their sales job. It fulfills their need by allowing them to have more time for themselves and for their families. People do like to work but they would rather have more free time for their families as opposed to spending more time working. Since this software is a productivity tool, it allows them to gain more customers, to help them find more customers enabling them to sell more and make more money. When the software is marketed this way as fulfilling those needs and providing the benefit of making more money and helping to increase sales efforts, then salespersons will want to buy the product and they do end up buying the software.

If you are marketing, towards senior citizens, any product or service that you offer to them that gives them the comfort of knowing that they are being taken care of and that they are being protected and watched over will sell very well. That product or service will allow the senior citizens to feel good and the need being fulfilled is that a person wants to be healthy, taken care of and protected. Whatever product or service you sell to a senior market would have to be something that would truly help them by either providing protection, insuring their health or safety, or keeping them in touch with their families. Senior citizens have a strong need as everyone does for having close relationships with other people.

Regardless of the market that you are serving, make sure to find products or services that hit the nail squarely on its head. Basically, your products or services must genuinely deliver and accurately fulfill the need in the market place that you are looking to serve. If you are able to accomplish this, you will have a very successful online business.

Chapter Five

When most people start an online business, they do not realize that most of the work is already laid out for them. They wrongly assume that they will need to start their business from scratch. By starting it from scratch, I mean that they will have to research fully the business before they are able to launch it. I am not contradicting what I said earlier since research is extremely important and you need to be willing to do a tremendous amount of research to have a successful online business. What I will show you in this chapter is how you can avoid and eliminate a lot of the research that you need to do by doing the following steps. The following strategies will only work if you have already done your basic research and it will work even better if you have done an extensive amount of research as suggested earlier in the book. Depending upon how much research you have done, the following strategy will only help your business even more.

The strategy that we will be discussing in this chapter is developing your marketing strategy based on your competitor's success. This strategy may seem simple, but you would be surprised at how many online entrepreneurs ignore this important strategy. You see, when you start a business, online or offline, a lot of the work has already been laid out for you. There have been pioneers who have already ventured into that business market and have already discovered through trial-and-error what works in that market. These people have already eliminated flawed marketing strategies. They have discovered which products or services sell well in the market and what prices they need to set for those products or services in order to have a large volume and make money at the same time.

Therefore, in order for you to have a successful online business, study what the pioneers have done. I once heard that the CEO of "Toys R Us" says the following in a class. "The difference between the veterans and the pioneers is that the pioneers have laid out the path but now they are lying on the ground with an arrow in their backs. The veterans are the people who came after the pioneers, developed what the pioneers had already established and were able to succeed." Even though you may only be starting your online business now and may only be a beginner, act as if you are a veteran. Study what the pioneers have already done and making notes and lists of their strengths and weaknesses. Make a list of what works for other online entrepreneurs and what does not work for them and then apply all of the information that you have learned.

In other words, instead of going ahead and playing around with your ad copy, instead of trying different pictures of the product by itself, show the product being used and picture people who have used the product. Instead of deciding what type of testimonials will help sell you products the best, trying to decide to vote for pictures or high impact testimonials online, trying to decide where to advertise your products online, use information provided by others. You do not need to do all of this by yourself because there have been other people who already spent countless hours and thousands of dollars if not hundreds of thousands of dollars testing everything out and have already determined what the best course of action would be for your business.

For instance, if you want to sell books online, even though you will face a tremendous amount of competition, you can succeed. You would succeed if you sell a highly specific type of book, meaning if you decided to sell books by competing head on with Barnes & Noble or Amazon you would have a very difficult time. They have many marketing dollars, an established online name, a good reputation, and as a starting business, you would find them very difficult to compete with other than to take customers away from them. However, on the other hand if you develop a "niche" online and for example you sell books catering to people who want to lose weight by eating Chinese food or books that cater to the market of people who are looking to lose weight but at the same time enjoy eating Chinese food, you will be aiming at a very narrow market. Since you will not have a lot of competition in that market which is very narrow and was overlooked by Barnes & Noble and Amazon as many other small niches are, you will be able to succeed.

If you want to sell books to this narrow market you have found, you still have all the big questions such as how to reach this market, how to advertise, how to write the text for the book, whether to put pictures of the books on the web site, whether to have testimonials from readers, whether to have the author review the book or write comments about the book so people can get more of an insight about the author of the book, or whether to post book reviews from other sources on your web site? In order to answer all of these questions, you do not need to do all of the research on your own. In this situation, you could actually look at the Barnes & Noble and Amazon websites to see how they sell books online. How do they advertise their books online? How do they describe the books that they sell? How do they solicit testimonials from their readers? Do they have an affiliate program? Do they use search engines? Do they advertise e-zines? Are they advertising offline? Are they allowing readers to post testimonials on books?

Using all of the information that has already been collected and tested in million dollar campaigns by the big booksellers, you can be ahead of the curve by now using all of that information that is publicly available in developing your own online business. Even though you are an upstart without the millions of dollars in research and advertising tools that Barnes & Noble and Amazon have, you could piggyback their success by copying their strategies and formulas and implementing those formulas into your own business.

As you can see, by closely studying what your competitors are doing in business, you are able to develop strategies and apply already proven strategies that work. I am sure that some of you remember a web site called "etoys.com". Etoys.com had a very interesting premise, which was very basic, and it seemed that it should have very easily worked out online. The premise it was working on was to have one destination where consumers could go online and purchase a wide array of toys. A consumer could walk this same way into Toys R Us or to KB Toys and purchase toys from a large array. Therefore, Etoys.com was hoping that people would come to the web site and purchase toys from them online. Now Etoys.com, as you may know, failed. Not only did they fail but also they went millions of dollars into debt. Remember, they had hundreds of millions of dollars at their disposal to develop their business and they simply burned up all of the investor money that they had without showing a profit and without having a solid business plan. They did not have any proof that the business was viable and that it could move towards profitability. As a matter of fact, I remember reading that it cost Etoys.com approximately $250.00 to acquire every customer that it had purchase from it. The theory behind Etoys.com marketing strategy was that they were willing to spend a lot of money to acquire a customer because once they a customer for a lifetime, that customer would make the money back for them that they had to spend. Meaning, they expected that $250.00 customer to buy so many toys that the profit generated from the purchases would surpass the cost and in the long run, they would make money from each customer. The problem with this was that just because they acquired a customer, there was no guarantee that the customer would buy from them again. As a matter of fact a customer who purchases toys is not looking for specialized products or services they are simply looking for a toy either for their own children or as a gift for someone else's child.

You should learn from the mistakes that Etoys.com made. The biggest mistake was that they spent too much money acquiring customers and that they counted on customers purchasing again. Instead, when you develop your strategy you should plan to have a long-term strategy and you should realize and take into account that the lifetime value of a customer is a lot more important than the profit that comes from the initial purchase. This does not mean that you should lose money in acquiring that customer and in producing that first order. On the other hand, you should be willing to have a small profit on the first order in exchange for establishing a good will relationship with the customer. This does not mean that you should give away your profits and sell to the customer at a loss because there is no guarantee that the customer will stay as your customer or will ever buy from you again.

Another mistake that Etoys.com made is that when they marketed themselves, they did not explain to the customers what made them special and explain to them why the customers should buy from them as opposed to the regular channels from which customers normally purchased. Amazon.com sells toys online as well as many other web sites that sell toys online and are able to thrive. They are able to thrive either because they already had a built in customer base or they were able to demonstrate to the customers that they could provide special types of products or services and that they were able to compete based on price. Competition based on price is an extremely dangerous practice, as we will discuss later. If you already have a built in customer base who is loyal to you, then you give the customer an extra incentive to buy from you by offering a special price on purchases. In this situation, you will be giving the customer a special price as far as purchasing a toy from you, then it does indeed pay to offer customers a very low price in order to motivate them to purchase from you.

There was another web site that at the beginning seemed to have a lot of potential but this web site also failed. Pets.com seemed to have a lot of potential being devoted towards selling everything that a pet owner might need ranging from pet supplies, collars, leashes and pet food. Pets.com also went under because they spent too much money acquiring customers and by advertising in places that were not directly targeted to its customer base. Meaning, if a customer in Arkansas saw an ad for Pets.com while surfing the web at a web site that catered towards antiques, then that customer might not be interested in anything that Pets.com had to offer, they may not have a pet. Even if they did have a pet, at that particular time the customer was not thinking about pets but rather he was thinking about antiques, which would make an antique web site the wrong place to advertise.

One important lesson that you can learn from Pets.com is that when you advertise online you need to advertise in targeted places that reach your intended customers. If you want to advertise on someone's web site, make sure that the web site is visited by your intended customers, and also that the customers are visiting the site for the same reason that they would also have visited your own web site. Pets.com would have been a lot more successful if they would have advertised specifically on pet related sites. Not only would they have reached customers who have pets but they also would have reached the customers at a time when they were thinking about their pets, which would have been the ideal time to convince them to purchase from Pets.com.

As you can see, there is a lot that you can learn from your competitors. As a matter of fact, the most you can learn in business is from the successful actions of your competitors and from the actions your competitors are taking that are not positive.

One question that arises is "What if you are starting out in a new "niche" that currently has no competition? Well on one hand, that is great because you will not have any competition and will be able to control the market until the competition arises. The dilemma is that you do not have any information from which to work. You cannot see what other people have done in the area in order to become successful and what mistakes they have made that you should avoid.

The first step in that type of situation is to find a similar niche that is either closely related or mirrors the area that you want to serve with the same customer characteristics with the same needs and benefits that they are looking to fulfill.

For instance, you want to sell painting supplies online and it happens to be that the type of painting supplies that you want to sell and the type of artists that you want reach are not currently being served. Let's say that you want to reach people who are specifically interested in painting Renaissance style painting using acrylic colors and that those artists specifically want to paint on paper canvases. That is a very specific target audience that you want to reach. While the traditional web sites are catering towards artists and people who like Renaissance style paintings but you are going beyond that and finding a very, very definite niche to which you want to cater, you will not have competition and will be able to control the market.

In this type of situation, what you would do is to look at web sites that cater to artists and similar niches. You may look at a web site that caters to artists who enjoy painting gothic paintings or you may look into European paintings. Regardless to which niche those online web sites are catering, as long as they are catering to artists and long as long as they are catering to a very specific type of artists, you can study how they are advertising, how they reach their customer base, and what the sales process is to convince their customer base to make a purchase from their web site. By comparing and contrasting your business effort to their business efforts, you can see what works and what does not work as well as what you need to avoid and what you need to do in order to succeed with your online business.

Remember, every niche has a counterpart. By this, I mean just as there is a niche of people who enjoys collecting old stamps there is also a niche of people who enjoys old magazines. While these two areas are clearly, separate issues but are similar in that they are both collectors. Each enjoys old collectibles that are no longer produced and they are both likely nostalgic and reflective in thinking about the past. They are also people who enjoy spending time looking at their collections. A magazine is meant to be read as is a stamp is meant to be viewed and enjoyed. They each conjure memories and have a place in history, signifying a defining moment about when and why they were each issued. As you can see, these are two separate niches sharing very similar characteristics in regards to the customers involved in those specific venues.

So if you were looking to start a web site selling to the same collectors who enjoy stamps from the early 1800's and are there are no similar websites which you can study, you could look at web sites that cater to people who like to read magazines from the same time period and those types of collectors will have similar characteristics as those you want to target. You can study the marketing efforts through any web sites that cater to the magazine collectors and you can then decide what you need to do in order to reach those collectors and what can you do to succeed by emulating the magazine web site that is reaching your customers. You can also study your competition by determining which competitors are managing the successful web sites you are studying by seeing which are the most successful and why they are the most successful. There could be many web sites catering to a specific niche. Even though Barnes&Noble.com and Amazon.com are clearly, the most successful online booksellers there are hundreds of thousands of other small web sites selling books. I think that you would agree with me that the most successful online sellers are these two major sites. Imagine the mistake made by someone deciding to only study a small online bookseller and not focus on Barnes&Noble.com or Amazon.com.

What if someone decided that he or she would rather follow the advice of a small online book site as opposed to the advice that would generate the success of the two large sellers? I hope that you would agree with me that this person would clearly be going down the wrong path. Rather they should be asking themselves, which are the best websites that cater to this niche. Which web sites seem to have the best and biggest customers? Which sites seem to have the best customer retention rate? A lot of this information is publicly available, testimonials are readily available on the web sites and reviews that readers have posted can be read regarding the web site you are studying. This will give you good information about how customers feel regarding the web site's ability to cater to their needs. If you want to have a good grasp on how this web site is doing type the name of the web site and into the Google search engine box and then look at web sites who review the site that you are studying. This way you can see if people are generally content or dissatisfied with the site you are examining. If you see that customers are generally very content with the web site that you are examining and there are, many people who write about the web site it will seem that this is a successful web site with a high level of customer retention rate.

Once you know that a specific web site is successful and if it is more successful than its competitors are then you will know that you should study that web site and see what is making it successful. As you study that web site, you need to determine where it is advertising. You can do this by searching online and sooner or later by visiting the categories that the web site is serving to see if it is promoting itself through an e-mail newsletter which is an e-zine, through a paperclip search engine, an affiliate program, offline advertising, untargeted banner ads, targeted banner ads joint ventures, third party endorsements or by testimonials. All of these marketing tools will be discussed later as well as how to apply them to your own business. As of now, you need to go online and make a list of how that successful web site is promoting itself online, how it is marketing itself to customers and how it is selling. You also need to write down how the site sells its products, meaning, what are the quantities that it sells per sale. Does it force customers to make a minimum purchase or allow them to order any number of units that want? Does the site offer free shipping or do they charge for shipping? Does the site subsidize the shipping? Is the web site competing based on price or based on service? Does the web site have a newsletter? Does it have a FAQ (frequently asked questions) section? Does it sell products or services by giving too much information or by eliciting curiosity?

Once you are able to have a clear grasp of what is allowing that web site to succeed then you will be able to adapt all of the information to your online web site and business venture. You will literally be years ahead of the game because you will be building upon the success of your competitors and of other successful web sites that have already made money in the market that you are looking to serve.

Therefore, you need to make it a part of your schedule to study your competition on a day-to-day basis, on a weekly basis, on a monthly basis and at any time a new competitor enters the market or a competitor leaves the market. You must be willing to study and come up with a conclusive answer as to why that competitor entering the market feels that it will be able to succeed and if it is introducing a new product into the market or if it has a better price than anyone else does. We all know that anytime a new business goes online that business wants to make money. That new online business would not think it could make money in the face of competition unless it believed that it clearly had something to place it at an advantage as compared to its competition. When you see a new business go online, you want to determine what factor it believes places it at an advantage and how you can copy that factor and put that element into your own business plan. Your business will become saturated with that advantage, you could prosper in the face of current competition, and the competition posed by the new site as well. If you see a web site that is doing very well that you did not notice before, you will want to study why that web site is doing well and what is enabling it to take more of the customer share away from the competition.

It you see a web site that unfortunately goes out of business or decides to no longer cater to the portion of the market to which you are catering you will also want to decide why this business is able to take those actions. Did the operators of the web site discover that it is simply too expensive to service the customers? Is it too difficult to deliver the products on a timely basis? Is shipping too expensive for customers? Is customer retention an issue?

Even if all of the issues that led that web site to decide to cease its operations are true, this does not mean that you have to let those issues discourage you. What you need to do is decide how to best address those issues and solve the problems and dilemmas that the operators of the site faced. Determine how you can overcome those problems and turn the situation around so that you can become successful in that area. Every problem, situation and challenge has a solution. It is only a matter of discovering that precise solution of choice. Those who do discover the solution are able to become successful online entrepreneurs. If you see a competitor of yours go out of business or ceases operations because it simply decides that it does not want to offer free shipping anymore and believes it cannot get the customers' business without offering free shipping, what you need to do is either raise your prices and still offer free shipping or deliver such a great customer service that your customers will not mind paying for shipping. If your customers demand free shipping and you need to charge for shipping to stay in business, you can tell customers that even though you are forced to charge for shipping, that you are charging a bare minimum of the costs and are enclosing free bonuses to compensate for the shipping fee.

Suppose you are selling a box of chocolates online and the box costs $39.95. The shipping cost for the chocolates is approximately $6.00. You have decided that you do not want to give free shipping any longer and you want to charge your customers the $6.00 but you are afraid that your they may not continue ordering from you any longer. The first thing that I will tell you is that as long as you can show your customers why your chocolates are such high quality that they should continue to order from you and should even be willing to spend more money than they ordinarily would, then your customers will buy from you. The problem is usually not the price or the cost to the consumers, the problem is that customers do not fully understand why they should buy from you and they do not have a high perception of the value that you are giving them. If you are able to deliver something to customers that will impress them by clearly communicating the high level of value that you are offering them, then the customers will not mind spending the money and will not mind spending even more money on your products and services than on lesser ones offered by competitors or other outlets. In this situation where you are sending out a box of chocolate and are charging $39.95 and you feel that on top of that price it is going to be just too expensive for your customers to spend an additional $6.00 on their chocolates, you could tell your customers that you will be giving them an extra small bonus box of chocolates to compensate them for the shipping cost. Now you could list that bonus box of chocolates as having a retail price of $12.95 and the actual cost of the bonus box may only cost you $1.00 to $2.00 because you can include chocolates that you bought from a closeout or any that were not selling or were moving slowly. In any event, you should only include a bonus of any kind that does not cost you much but has a high value perception attached to it. When people hear what bonus that you are giving them, they will be very excited about that bonus. I have seen very successful online marketing campaigns that relied heavily on the bonuses that they were giving away. Not only did they promote their bonuses heavily and demonstrate the great value of their bonuses but they promoted their bonuses in a way that their customers looked forward to receiving those bonuses so much that in many instances they bought the products or services simply to receive the bonuses.

The Bank of New York was able to attract many customers to the bank and had many customers open up bank accounts by offering to give them a free microwave oven. The microwave had a retail value of $59.00. In exchange for opening a new account with a minimum opening balance of $10,000.00, the customers would receive the microwave oven. The interest that customers were being given on the $10,000.00 was about ½% less than the interest that they were receiving from another bank which meant that the first year the customers were receiving 3 ½% on their money instead of 4% or instead of $400.00 in interest they only received $350.00. However, they were so excited to receive the microwave that they were willing to forego a certain portion of their interest in order to receive the bonus. The Bank of New York was very smart because the microwave oven only cost them $15.00 to $20.00 so they actually came out ahead. Not only was Bank of New York able to pay less for the money that it was borrowing from its depositors but was able to attract many customers by offering a free bonus, which seemed to be very valuable. That bonus was indeed very valuable because after all because it was a $59.00 microwave which the customers wanted to enjoy having but which actually cost the bank was only $15.00 to $20.00 per new customer.

Think about how much ahead the bank was in this situation. Instead of having to pay the interest of $400.00 at that time for a $10,000.00 deposit, as other banks had to pay, it only paid out interest of $350.00. The bank saved $50.00 and out of that savings, $15.00 went into the cost of the microwave, which provided a net profit of $35.00 per new depositor. If the bank opened 5,000 new accounts with this promotion, we are talking about $75,000.00 profit that was generated simply by offering a free bonus that seemed to have a high level of value to the customers. Remember, most people might have just opened a $10,000.00 bank account, but once they had already opened up an account that they might even deposit $20,000.00 or $30,000.00 in that account. Think of how much more the Bank of New York saved in interest by being able to pay a lower interest rate to these depositors in exchange for a microwave oven. If someone had a $30,000.00 deposit in the bank, that person would receive $350.00 in interest for every $10,000.00, which is $1,050.00 total interest on that sum. The Bank of New York would have been required to give these people $1,200.00 on that same $30,000.00 deposit if it had been required to pay the same interest rate that other banks were giving at that time. By offering the free microwave oven, the Bank of New York was able to save $150.00 on those specific types of deposits.

With your online business, you always want to give people bonuses that have a high level of value for your customers even though the bonuses did not cost you much. Do you remember how we have already discussed the needs of people and the benefits that people are looking to receive? It does not matter if the item that you are giving to your customers costs you a lot of money and it does not even matter if you got the item free. What matters is whether your customer has a need for the item and whether the customer would enjoy the benefits that the item would provide. As long as the bonus you are offering fulfills those two criteria, you will have many customers willing to do business with you just to receive the bonus. You can assume that they will be strongly influenced by the bonus and will make their buying decision based on the bonuses that they will be receiving. Remember, when they compare doing business with you to doing business with your competitors if you are giving them a bonus that fulfills a need and provides a benefit they will opt for doing business with you. Even if your products are more expensive or if you charge for shipping while your competitors do not charge for shipping, people will still order from your web site as long as the bonus you are offering has a higher level of value to them than the money that are spending.

At one of the websites that I once had, I charged for an e-book, which was a downloadable book that people could read directly from their computer. I charged $97.00 for the e-book while my nearest competitors charged only $50.00 for a similar e-book. The reason that I was able to sell more copies than my competitors were able to sell is that the book I marketed my e-book in a way that people understood that their needs would be fulfilled and that they would receive the benefits that they wanted. I provided bonuses enclosed in the sales process that were extremely valuable to them, fulfilled their needs, provided benefits and was something that they definitely wanted. The purchase was presented as being worth more than the money-saving factor of buying from my nearest competitor. So by offering bonuses to my customers that fulfilled a need and gave them benefits that they could really use, and by showing them how the bonuses were worth more to them than the savings of buying from my competitors, I was able to become successful in selling my e-book. The bonuses took away the customer anxiety caused by my competitor's price of nearly half the amount I was charging. I made sure that my customers were always assured they were being compensated with bonuses that they would enjoy and could use, while at the same time using the bonuses to distinguish me from my competition. Many of my customers ordered the e-book just to get the bonuses because they may have determined that in their situation those bonuses were very valuable to them.

Always make sure that you are offering something to your customers that not only distinguishes you from your competition but it is something that your customers will truly enjoy and they genuinely need. As we discussed in this chapter in order to know what makes a successful online business distinguish itself from a failing online business, you need to study your competitors, you need to read up on web sites that went out of business to determine why they went out of business and you also need to study successful websites to see what elements help those websites succeed. When you apply the strategies that you are learning, then you too will have the opportunity of having an extremely successful online business.

Chapter Six

In order for you to have a successful online business, you must have what I will call the success factor. The success factor is the element that will enable you to succeed by distinguishing your business from other online businesses. In other words, the success factor is going to be the distinguishing factor that clearly puts you at an advantage as compared to other online businesses that occupy the same niche that you are looking to serve. If you are looking to serve a niche that has no competitors, then that in itself is your success factor. What you are attempting to do with an online business is develop for yourself a success factor, or in other words, to develop a market position strategy that will enable you to rise over the competition or to put yourself in a situation where you have no competition.

You see Barnes&Noble.com and Amazon.com both have two different success factors that they each use to steal business away from each other and to develop a good amount of business for their bottom line. Barnes&Noble.com has a unique success factor. Their success factor is the ability to allow customers to pick up their orders at any retail location. This means simply that a Barnes&Noble.com customer who has purchased a book online can opt to pick up the purchase at the closest retail location. While most customers are looking to benefit from the service of having the book delivered to their door, many customers like the fact that they will not have to pay for shipping, they will not have to stand in line because their book will be waiting at the counter, and they still get to enjoy the savings that are offered through the web site as opposed to ordering a book directly at the bookstore or searching the shelves for the book.

The Amazon.com success factor is the free shipping that it offers on all of its orders. Customers know that if they order a minimum amount of books, which usually comes out to be $25.00, they will enjoy the free shipping. That is not a hard minimum to reach because all it usually takes is the purchase of one to two books.

Therefore, you see the two companies have very different success factors but they use both of them to distinguish themselves from their competition. In order for you to succeed online, you also have to develop your own success factor that will allow you to rise above the competition in the eyes of your customers. A good success factor in the service business could be to offer a free e-book that will give other people guidance in how to benefit the most from the service you are providing. If you are offering a product then you can offer free shipping except that success factor is already widely available and has been copied by many other entrepreneurs. You need to be able to develop a success factor that others have not yet developed.

One type of success factor that you could develop is that of giving free bonuses as we have already mentioned. You can offer an extra 5% to 10% worth of merchandise with every order. Instead of competing in price, you are then delivering more to the customer for the same price. In other words, the customer is now receiving more for his money. That is something, which will set you apart in the customer's mind from another provider of the same product.

There are many types of success factors. One success factor that you can offer is free consulting along with the purchase of a product or service that you are selling on your web site. This is a great success factor because once a customer has decided to buy your product or service they have expressed their need for it, they have expressed their desire to receive the benefits that your product or service offers, and now they will clearly want to enjoy being able to experience the maximum benefit from the product or service that you are offering. The free consulting will enable them to experience the benefit. Therefore, if you have a web site that caters to the business-to-business market in which your web site is selling to other businesses or is selling to people who want to start or run their own businesses, the free consulting is a great success factor. This is true because not only do most web sites that cater to other businesses not offer free consulting, as a matter of fact, if they do offer consulting, they charge for it. Most business-to-business online web sites do not offer any type of consulting at all. You can see how you are already distinguishing yourself by offering free consulting. The reason why free consulting is such a perfect success factor for business-to-business web sites is because the very nature of people in business is that they are always seeking more information, new ideas and strategies to grow their business and help them out pace their own competition. If you offer a product or service that is catering to the business-to-business market on your web site, remember that the customer's need is to make more money and the benefit for which he is looking is the benefit that comes from making more money. Their needs could be those of someone who is actually in business for himself or herself and wants to be able to spend more time with their family or wants to be able to better support their family. The benefit would be the luxury of making more money and the things they can do with that money.

If you properly market your success factor by explaining it correctly, then people might actually purchase your product or service just to have access to your free consulting. For example, you might offer an advertising package that has the following characteristics. For $1,999.00 a customer can buy a package that includes four ads that are specifically created for the customer's marketing campaign, ad copy for the web site and for the customer's offline advertising, information on 10 different sources of where to place these advertisements and when the ads should be placed. Now that is a great advertising package for people in business because everyone in business needs to advertise and wants to advertise so that they can increase their business, gain more customers and make more money, after all everyone goes into business to make more money. If you offer free consulting it will excite your customers because not only will they be receiving your great advertising package but through your consulting they will benefit from having you will actually guide them step by step in placing the ads, explaining the best times to use the ads, advising them how to use the ads productively, and also exploring what changes they can make in order to increase their effectiveness. You could give them ideas on how to follow up on leads that they receive from the ads, how to close sales, which products to actually offer people who call to inquire about the ads, and whether they should send out a brochure, e-mail or catalog. There are many types of consulting that you can do along with this type of an offer. As you can see the business-to-business market place is perfect for free consulting offers because everyone in business desperately needs information in order to increase his or her business and to be able to continue to grow. Your success factor can also be similar if you have a retail web site or one that caters to the consumer market. Let's say that you have a web site that is a membership based web site, which for $20.00 per month allows your customers access to the latest recipe-posting menu on your site. Suppose you post a new recipe every day and you have different categories of recipes such as for weight loss, fine dining, business lunches, anniversaries, weddings, specific holidays, religious holidays or any other special occasion. This could be a great product to sell online because people enjoy cooking and eating and being exposed to new recipes that they can use for various specific occasions. Imagine if you were to offer free consulting in this situation. What would this free consulting consist of to present it value to your customers? Along with a membership, you could offer the right to contact you via e-mail once a week to discuss any recipes that you have posted and have you answer any questions that they have regarding any of the recipes posted. For instance if you post a recipe on a special pizza sauce that consists of olives and mushrooms along with great herbs and spices that are only available from Indian sources, then people could contact you and discuss with you the best herbs to use, the best way to prepare the sauce, and your recommendations about additional ingredients to make the sauce tastier. As you can see, even something as simple as recipes provides a niche in order to give people information and to offer free consulting to people. Even though consulting is only usually associated with large corporations and high-end million dollar businesses, every person needs consulting on some basis and every person has some type of consulting to offer. The word consulting could be changed to "advice" or "learning". Whatever translation of the word that you use, keep in mind that in every online situation where a customer buys from you, there is an opportunity to offer free consulting and even fee-based consulting if you should choose.

As you develop your online business, study what your competitors are doing and develop your own ideas about your success factor for your business. Think about the true needs that people have in the market that you are serving, what the true benefits are that they are looking to obtain from your product or service, and then start deciding what you can offer as a free bonus. If not a free bonus, it could be an add-on service or product for which you will charge but is distinguishable from what your competitors offer. This way you will be able to develop a success factor that will cause customers to be drawn to your site and to become long-term customers of your business. By developing a success factor, you will be emulating many large established online companies such as eBay, Amazon, Yahoo! and many other lesser known but still successful websites.

Chapter Seven

This chapter will discuss the importance of using a business plan for your online business. An online business requires a special amount of diligence and certain organizational skills in order to be successful. When you go online with a business, you are going to be facing not only many components and facets, both internally and externally with which you must deal, but you will also be dealing with issues that are literally developing and presenting themselves at the speed of light. Think about this…the Internet is a "real time" business tool, a communication tool. Everything that happens online happens in an instant. If someone posts a negative feedback regarding your site, you need to be able to deal with it instantly. If a product that you are selling is out of stock, you need to be able to make adjustments instantly. If a product becomes available or if you are able to make a good purchase and you want to offer those products or services to your customers you can do it immediately. As you can see, there are many factors of an online business and those factors are occurring and changing in a rapid manner unlike an offline business.

Therefore, in order for you to run a successful online business you will need to have a business plan, which we will call an online business plan, which needs to take into account all facets of your business. It will need to include product procurement, where you will be purchasing the products that you will be reselling, how you will be developing the services that you are offering, how you will be marketing the products and services that you offer, how you will advertise the products and services, how you plan to sell the products and services, where you plan to market and advertise, how you plan to deliver the product or service, how you plan to follow up with consumers, and how to develop and maintain lists of prospects and customers. You will need to be able to determine how you will deal with issues such as customer complaints or returned items. You need to decide how to reward good customers and how you will continue to find new opportunities to develop further the business. As you can see, many factors need to be addressed in running an online business. If you want a successful online business, then you want to be able to diffuse or address all of these factors and stay on top in your market, so you will need a business plan, which will specifically address all of the issues.

What a business plan is basically is an instruction manual, which is being set up specifically to help you run your business. This instruction manual will allow you to be able to consult it so you can always look at what you should be doing. Let's say that a situation arises and you have a question and it is something with which have not dealt previously. Even though your business plan may not specifically cover the exact issue for this type of question, it can do is show you how should deal with a similar situation. When you look at your business plan, what also takes place is that your ideas, strategies, and inspirations become concrete formulas that you can follow instead of only being thoughts in your head. It is similar to setting up a model airplane. When you set up a model, you may understand the basic idea behind setting up the plane and you may understand what tools you will need to put it together. You also may have basic understanding of which pieces need to be glued together first. If you want to get the details right and succeed at assembling the model plane, you will want to make sure to follow the instructions for assembly in the manual that is enclosed.

The same is true of your online business. If you want your online business to not only reach its goal but also to likewise reach the goal in a timely and efficient manner then you want the end results of that business to be what you envisioned. You may even want the results to surpass what you envisioned, so then you need to be able to have an instruction manual to help guide you in running your business clearly. This is the true value of a business plan.

If you do not feel you are ready to formulate your own business plan, then I would suggest that you hire a consultant who can either formulate a business plan for you or could consult with you and guide you through the formulation process. The consultants will charge anywhere from a few hundred dollars or up to $20,000.00 to formulate a business plan. That is quite an expensive proposition for a starter business and I do not recommend it. The only alternative to using a consultant is sitting down and forcing yourself to make your own business plan. I can guarantee you that a business plan will be extremely helpful.

What happens many times in business if that when an individual is excited and looks forward to running his or her business they are full of ideas and inspiration and understand what they want to do. However, as they become involved with the business and many mundane issues arise, they can lose focus of their actual goals. Then they become bogged down in the details of running the business and forget about their goals and their objectives. The goals of course are the long-term results and the objectives are the short-term things that you want to accomplish, in other words, the short-term benchmarks that you want to reach.

Now if you have various objectives and various goals, it will be very difficult to keep track of all these goals and objectives unless you have then written down on paper. Once you have the goals and objectives written down, you might then know what you must do to reach those objectives. As you become involved in the business on a daily basis, you may forget how you planned to reach those objectives. Therefore, you want to be able to expand your knowledge and expand on what you can do with your business. In order to do this you need to have all of these concrete objectives, goals, and formulas written down as far as exactly what you need to do to reach your objectives. If you decide that you want to advertise your web site in a local trade journal that caters to your market then you should write it down. Not only write this down in your business plan but also write down which trade journals in which you want to advertise. You will also write in your plan that you want to look for other avenues in which to advertise. Further, you want to note in your business plan how you would go about finding those other avenues to advertise. The reason that you want to write down every step of your business is because when you run your web site and you are involved in the tasks of developing the web site such as writing ad copy, photographing your products, posting those photographs on your site, advertising and marketing your site, contacting prospective customers or responding to customer inquiries, you can become distracted.

There are so many issues that are taking place, tasks that need to be done, and business functions that need to take place when one runs an online business that you could forget all of your different objectives. You could even forget how you were going to reach those objectives. I will be the first one to admit that sometimes when I am running my business and I have an idea into which I start delving that I sometimes forget exactly my end goal from getting in lost in the forest where I cannot see the trees. Think about it for a minute, you could spend so much time and effort trying to achieve a certain goal that you forget the different objectives that were going to lead to the goal.

If you have two or three websites and two of them are profitable while one is not, instead of spending countless hours and funds trying to make the one web site profitable, ask yourself about the actual goal you want to accomplish. Your goal was to have a profitable online business. Therefore, you may decide to leave this one unprofitable web site, close it down, and launch another web site that can become profitable. In order for all of this to take place you will need to have a guide for yourself steering you along the way and reminding you of what your true goals are and what objectives would allow you reach the goals. In order for you to be successful with your online business, you will need to have a business plan that is growing continuously. By this, I mean that as your business progresses and as your business changes, you want to be able to adapt to changes in your business plan. If you realize that you need to go in a different direction in order to make money online or in order to expand your online business, that is fine…but include it in your business plan and write in your plan how you now hope to reach your goals and how you hope to increase your revenue or how can develop a secondary online revenue source.

Further, the business plan is great for you because you may have new ideas on how to expand your online business. You may be reading a business magazine or reviewing the success of an online entrepreneur and afterwards you may want to incorporate those ideas into your own online business. If you have a business plan and the plan is flexible, you can take those ideas that you have learned and include them in the business plan and adjust the plan accordingly. Now you will have an instruction book or a guide that incorporates the ideas that you are continuously learning through reading, meeting with other people and networking and you can use the ideas to expand your online business.

As you can see, every time that you interact with people and every time you read and investigate online opportunities and every time that you study your competitors, you are going to be receiving ideas and coming up with new strategies and concepts that help you develop tips and secrets that will help you succeed. Instead of letting all of those concepts and ideas, tips and strategies go to waste since you might soon forget them after you put down that publication, write them all down. Therefore, even if those ideas are not applicable today but could become applicable three months from now or six months from now, you will be able to draw upon those ideas and capitalize on them. Even if your online business is not yet up to the point at which it needs to use the strategy which you have learned from interacting with another online entrepreneur, when your business gets to the point where it can benefit from these strategies you will be able to look at your business plan, read the strategy and be reminded of the details, how it is meant to be applied, and how it could deliver maximum results for you. Then you will be able to include that strategy into your plan and into your actual business. Having a business plan is great because it keeps you disciplined and reminds you of what you set out to do and how you have decided to accomplish your goals. The business plan allows you to incorporate new ideas and strategies for reviewing later as you continuously guide yourself through the business whether you are receiving a new idea, strategy or concept. You might want to attend a class in online business and may learn something in that class that gives you another solid idea for your business.

Think about how many great ideas you have throughout your lifetime and how many times you forget an idea, which later there is an occasion when you could have used that idea, but its time has passed. Instead of letting this happen, a business plan will allow you to have a place where you can record all of your ideas. Anytime that you are inspired you will the opportunity to write down the ideas and keep them as a reference and as a record for your future use.

As an online entrepreneur, you want to make sure that you have a set pattern that you can follow, a set system in which you can operate consistently. Otherwise, there are so many other places where you could advertise online and so many ways to market a business and many different types of customer approaches that you can take. If you do not have a definite system to follow you will become lost and confused forgetting when you should be following which ideas. You will end up trying so many different advertising methods that you really should not be trying. When you have a business plan, it also helps you make note of which ideas work for you, and which strategies are the best to follow, and tips you received that you should avoid.

If you have a business plan and you list twenty different ways that you plan to market your business and you discover that only three of those methods are helping your business grow, then you cross off the other seventeen leaving only the three methods that are actually helping your business grow. Let's say that you focus on those three methods and as you are running your business, you see that one method works better when you modify it in a certain way. You can make a notation and follow that method the next time, making sure to have that notation in place on your plan so that you will know to follow the method a certain way. The same is true for any type of business concept, method, or strategy that you want to follow. As you see the method in action, you actually will see which method works best for you, its strengths and weaknesses and modify your methods on paper. If you do not modify them on paper, in addition to modifying them when you actually take action, the next time around you may forget what needs to be modified and you will make the same mistakes that you made previously. So in order to break that cycle, you want to be able to have everything written down on paper so that you can continuously monitor the progress of your online business. You can determine what works in your business and what does not work. You could focus on the actions that are actually leaning towards making money online.

I am sure that if you go through a simple search online of all the different online marketing methods and advertising methods that are available you will notice that there are thousands of web sites available. Each one promises you to bring customers to your site, to effectively market your products and services, and create your brand awareness within the minds of consumers. There are marketing web sites that will help you establish an online presence in the market with which you want to deal. Many of these offerings are going to be legitimate and many of those web sites might actually work. If you keep trying different service there will be no end to it. Would not it be better to try a few of those services and keep a notation of which ones work for you, what you gain from each service and what you lose from each service. Therefore, the next time that you want to do another marketing or advertising campaign you can look back at your business plan and see which service you should use. You might find three, four or even ten different services, which can help you. At the same time, you may find only one or two services that actually help you in the certain areas in which you actually need help. Why should you use all ten services if they do not help you specifically? So by having everything written down in your business plan you are able to remember what you should be doing and with whom you should be dealing.

Another benefit of having a business plan is that when you actually run a marketing campaign with a service provider, you can see the benefits of having run your campaign with that service provider and you can also see when it could have been improved. What was lacking with that provider? When you run your next campaign, you can contact that provider and tell them what was lacking and what needs to be done to correct the situation. Whatever that service provider did to provide benefits to you should also be increased on your behalf.

All of these steps can only be taken when you have a clear strategy and a deliberate method that allows you to collect all the information, analyze that information and then act upon its results. If you read any respectable business book and you speak to any respectable business owner each will tell you that they had a business plan. Many of them might not have actually written down the plan on paper but you will notice when comparing two similar types of business people, no matter how successful they are, that the one with the business plan, formal or informal plan, even if it only consists of some rules or guidelines, as compared to the one with no business plan at all, that the person with the complete plan will be the more successful. This is because the person with the business plan keeps his or her focus on the objectives and the goals that must be met. They have a record of from whom they buy, to whom they sell, what they sell, how they sell it, how they price, it, and how they market and advertise it. They have a plan, which entails how they will continue to look into finding better and additional suppliers and how they will continue to look for and find more customers in both quantity and quality. All of this is done by developing a business plan that encompasses every area of the business in which you will be dealing.

Chapter Eight

In this chapter, we will discuss the power of outsourcing and why outsourcing is essential for running a successful online business. Before we can discuss the need for outsourcing and the tremendous benefits that outsourcing provides for an online business, we have to discuss exactly what we mean by outsourcing. Outsourcing is the process of delegating tasks to another party who will complete those tasks on behalf of the business owner. In other words, outsourcing is having a task that needs to be done and finding someone else, either an individual or a business to do that task on your behalf. The reason that it is extremely important in an online business to outsource as much as you can is because there are so many issues that need to be addressed and those issues are constantly changing. Online businesses need to adapt to those issues but instead of the owner of the online business being bogged down with all of the details that arise a more prudent solution is to proceed in finding people who can be involved with those various tasks. The owner of the online business can choose to either hire employees and/or consultants or secure the services of independent contractors.

For example, you need to design a web site for your online business. This web site is going to be one the first things that your customers will see and is the medium by which your customers will interact with you. You need to make sure to have a very professional appearing web site. Even if you have HTML experience and know how to design a web site, it is still preferable to find an expert who can deliver a professionally designed web site that will impress all of your prospects and will turn your prospects into customers. You can spend weeks and months learning how to design a professional web site. You could spend hours and hours of revamping your site and adding nice features to the site and as you learn more techniques in terms of designing web sites, you could make improvements to the site. You could put up the site and through trial and error, you could see if you have developed a professional looking site. Your other option is to find someone who is already an expert in designing websites and outsource the work to this individual and let that person produce your web site, which will be ready for business in a short period. If there is something that you want to change or modify on the site, you can have this web designer do the modification for you or add any features that you desire without your having to be bogged down in the hours and hours that it would take you to do the work.

Think about this, even if it costs you more money to hire a web designer you would save a considerable if not enormous amount of time, which translates into money. How does it translate into money? If you create your own web site, it would take you a month to do properly and another month to get it to the point where customers can purchase from you. If you pay a site developer to do the work, it would be ready in a week. Think about the three-week period in which you would be missing customer orders by doing the site yourself. On the other hand, if you have a designer you will gain because in those three weeks you will have plenty of orders coming in to pay the designer. As you can see, having a web designer saves you time and that time translates into revenue from customers who can immediately start ordering from your site. When you have a web designer, it frees up all of your time to manage and run the business.

Another task that should be outsourced is the writing of ad copy for your site. You of course will try to develop ad copy for your site by writing copy and studying the best methods of writing ad copy. You could have a professional write ad copy that will work for you. I have seen professional ad copy pull in a conversion ratio of as high as 10% while ad copy that is written by a non-professional may not have a conversion ratio at all. A conversion ratio is how many prospects are converted into customers. If you have 100 visitors to your web site and you have a professional write your ad copy for you and they can deliver a 2% conversion ratio that means for every 100 visitors two will become customers. If on the other hand you try to write the ad copy yourself and you are a non-professional ad sales writer then you may have a 0% conversion ratio or it may be as low as ½% which means that out of every 100 prospects who see your site you may not have any customers and it will actually take 200 visitors to your site to produce one customer.

Look at the difference between having one customer for every 200 visitors as opposed to having up to five customers for every 100 visitors. The difference is dramatic, especially when you do not just have 100 visitors to your site. What if you have 1,000 visitors to your site or 10,000 visitors? Popular web sites that have a developed presence online, a good reputation and a strong following sometimes have upwards of millions of hits per month. Think about the difference in that in those terms.

An online expert told me that Amazon.com has a conversion ratio of 8% meaning that for every 100 visitors it receives, eight of them buy books. Think of how many millions and millions of visitors that they receive every day and every month. Think how many visitors that E-bay has every day and every month. Having ad copy that converts and turns your ads into customers is extremely important. Instead of your spending the time developing ad copy and trying to formulate the ad copy yourself, have a professional write the ad copy for you even if there is an expense so that you will start pulling in results immediately.

What areas should you outsource? Well, if you want to develop a marketing strategy develop a basic strategy, which you then have a professional review so that they can actually advise you whether you are headed in the right direction. Instead of you trying your marketing strategy by trial and error, you can actually have a professional review your marketing strategy, consult with you and make certain that you are going in the right direction. This person has more experience because he has dealt with many other customers who are also in the same situation as you and he has already tested many other marketing strategies. This marketing consultant knows what works and what does not work. As an online entrepreneur, you want to use every resource available to you.

Outsourcing does not always mean hiring an individual. Sometimes it can be using expert advice that is available publicly or privately. You can get the information by subscribing to a web site, reading a book or visiting a library. In a way, you are outsourcing the collection of information so that instead of your having to find the information on your own you are finding sources for the information. The more that you can outsource means the more time you will have to devote to the actual running of the business. The more that you can outsource means the more free time that you will have for yourself. This means that as you are using other people and other companies with other skills to handle the functions of your business, you may end up deciding to start a secondary business. You could even start a third business because your goal is to make money.

If the people are already, handling one business who have been designated different tasks you can devote your time to managing a second venture. As you outsource tasks for your second online business, you can move on to the third business. I know of successful online entrepreneurs who have ten different online businesses because they have learned how to outsource every task in which they do not personally have to be involved.

Another great task that should be outsourced is order fulfillment. This is done by having a company or individual actually processing your orders, collecting payment for the orders, sending them out, and insuring that the customer receives the order. There are firms that do order fulfillment only for as little as $5.00 per order and some for $1.00 per order depending upon what they are handling. As you develop your online business, you should look into order fulfillment outsourcing because it is truly cost effective and can help you in not being bogged down with your actual business and being able to manage the larger scope while other people fulfill the small tasks that are more cumbersome and need to be done.

Other tasks can be outsourced such as actual sales. If you want to have other people selling your products and services for you or bringing customers to your site, you can develop an affiliate system. Other people are compensated for either bringing prospects or actual customers to your site in this system. Later on, we will fully discuss in detail what is entailed in setting up an affiliate program. For now, you need only keep in mind that this is one great way to outsource the sales component of your business.

Now we have discussed how to outsource web site design, marketing, sales and order fulfillment. If you do not want to spend heavily on any of these functions you can find a college student, retiree or someone who stays at home and is looking for secondary income and happily become involved with your business for the money and also simply for the sake of being involved. Many web sites allow you to find people to whom you can outsource work to such as

Officemoonlighter.com, Creativemoonlighter.com and Businessmoonlighter.com that are all sites at which you can post projects and have people submit bids or proposals on them. When you go to these sites, you post your project regardless of what it is and then service providers bid on the project. They contact you and submit a bid in which they offer to complete your project for a certain fee. You review the bids and proposals and then determine the best person to work for you.

Let's say that you have a project concerning writing ad copy for your site. You post a job on Cfficemoonlighter.com and people bid on completing your project. This way you can get the best person to do the work for the most cost effective price. By following these steps, you will be able to develop leads on people who are willing to do the work for you at a cost effective basis. You can also review all of their resumes and see what makes them successful people in their own fields and decide if they have a quality resume and relevant experience to merit consideration for your project. Instead of hiring people with whom you are not familiar, you can establish business relationships with professionals by sending an e-mail, calling and talking to them on the phone, and reviewing other projects on which they have worked until you are sure that they can deliver what your business needs to succeed.

Another reason why outsourcing is so important is that if you do not learn to outsource, you will end up becoming an employee of your own business. By this, I mean that you will become proficient and even an expert at running certain parts of your business and that is all you that will end up accomplishing. In effect, you will be working for your business as if you were working for any other employer. When you work for someone else, you have certain tasks and goals that you must accomplish. When you work for yourself and you run your online business, you do not want to be required to focus on certain tasks and goals to the detriment of the overall picture. You do not want to be bogged down with working but rather you want to be managing your business so that it will grow and prosper. What you need to focus on is how to find other people to become the workers for your online business so you can focus on earning money from opportunities and finding additional opportunities. In turn, you will be developing methods for extracting more revenue from your current online revenue sources. At the same time, you want to develop methods for reducing expenses and growing your business to the next level. If you do not outsource routine tasks, you will not be able to do any of the things that we are discussing. The reason is that the majority of your time will be spent with basic functions that are important for running a business but which are not the basic functions that will deliver money into your pocket and make you rich. You always want to be involved in tasks that actually add to the bottom line. If a task does not actually put money in your pocket, then that task is not important in the sense of something in which you should be involved. On the other hand, if the task is important for your business to run and make money but does not directly make money, then you should either hire an employee or find an independent contractor to be involved with that task.

For example, a web site needs to be posted so that you do not have to buy a server to host your own web site. This would be very expensive and it would not make sense for you to spend the time to host a web site and deal with the problems that arise as a host. Instead, what you would do is to find a service provider that specializes in hosting web sites. The same is true for writing ad copy or promoting your site, developing an affiliate network, or finding products or services to sell. Any time that you can find some one to do a task for your business, it frees up your time to move on to the next task. Multinational companies are built this way. It always hires managers at every level to be responsible for different functions of the business. The manager on top of that manager is able to focus on the bigger picture. Then there is another manager who focuses on an even bigger picture until reaching the CEO who supervises the managers at every level. The CEO is then able to manage the overall direction of the company. You will not find the CEO working at the retail level of the store and you will not find the CEO of Amazon.com putting books in the mail.

Chapter Nine

As we discussed in the previous chapter the importance of outsourcing your work cannot be understated. Regarding the issue of having a web site developed for you by a professional, it is important that the person to whom you outsource will save you the time of attempting to do it yourself and at the same time create a site that will appear professional. This brings us to the next important point about online business ventures.

In order to be able to have a professional appearance you need your site designed by someone who is professional. This way it will give people the impression that you are an established business and are successful. The reason that this is important is because people like to deal with established businesses and with those that they perceive to be successful. The reasoning behind this is that if other customers enjoy dealing with a certain business that is successful then they will also enjoy dealing with you. In effect, if people see an online business with a lot of customers that has a good reputation they will understand that the reason they have the good number of customers is because they are delivering great products or quality services at a reasonable cost and the service is of superior worth.

You want to project the image of being a professional who is successful and having a good customer base with a strong online presence. By having this strong presence you want to make sure to distinguish your web site from all of the mom-and-pop-shop sites even though many of the sites that look professional are actually run by mom-and-pop operations. Many large corporate websites do not look professional at all and actually give the impression of being run by mom-and-pop operations or amateurs.

In order to succeed you need your customers to interact with you. When your customers look at your web site for the first time they will make a decision within 15 seconds whether they should continue investigating your site or simply move on with the click of a button. Remember how easy it is for someone who is surfing the Internet to go from site to site by merely clicking the back button and going back to the prior search or just entering a new address and leaving that site. Unless you give your customers a compelling reason to stay on your site and continue investigating it they will not stay. You also need to be able to show perspective customers and your current customers that you are a credible online business and that you are here to stay. Therefore, they probably won't consider buying from other competitors or even investigating other sources of the products and services that your offer because if you are going to be there for the long term then there is no reason for them to have to start looking for other sources of merchandise or services.

How do you convey all of this in 15 seconds through your web site? First, you have the site developed by a professional who has a good level of experience and can formulate a strategy for setting up your site with the look of a professional design. This does not mean that you cannot use a low cost source to produce your site. By this I mean a high school student, a college student or someone who took a few classes in Web Design could be effective low cost sources worth your consideration. Regardless of the years of expertise that the person has, and the educational background as related to web design, whether their work is of a professional caliber is the real issue you will want to consider. Therefore, do not attempt to save money by simply looking for a student to design your site or having a relative design it for you. If you concentrate only on saving money when it comes to site design you will have a very poor quality site that will leave a bad impression with your visitors. On the other hand, if you do find that student or relative who does have a high level of expertise when it comes to web design then you should definitely consider using this source for designing your web site.

The first thing that you need to learn from this chapter is that you must to use a professional to design your site. A professional can either be someone who has years of web site design experience and a high level of education concerning online design or it can be someone who simply can show you examples of other sites that they have designed. These sites should have a very professional appearance and should have been proven in attracting visitors and converting them into actual customers.

One important thing to remember is that today there are many tools available online to help design sites. There are many websites that will allow you to design and create a site free of charge. Should you use these sites? I would strongly recommend against using them for this reason. Think of all the other hundreds and thousands of people who are using those free services to set up their sites. Even though those sites offer different templates, which are the building blocks that build a site, there are only so many combinations available for your selection. For example, let's say that 1,000 people use the same web site creation service that is offered by a hosting company that wants to attract customers by allowing them to create a free site if they continue to host the site on their free service. This is a fine business premise but the end result is not in your favor because when you create your site along with the other 1,000 people, all of the sites will be very similar looking. Even if there are different colors or slightly different styles, there will still be many similarities. Upon comparing your site to others where both of you are offering the same products or services people will see no difference and they will simply assume that you are another small operation. If someone goes to a "cookie cutter site" which is what I consider one created free by one of these online services, and then they go to your site which is professionally designed your site will immediately stand out even if you are offering the same products and services as the other sites.

What you can do, and I definitely recommend that you should do this, is to advise your web site designer of all the free tools that are available online. Many web site design tools are free online and are great if used individually from the rest of the package. For example, there is one great tool, which I strongly recommend, that should be included and it is an auto responder tool. We will discuss later in detail what an auto responder tool is but basically, it allows you to send automatic e-mails in response to e-mails that your site receives. We will further go into detail discussing how you can use this tool to capture more visitors, turn visitors into customers and increase your sales. As of now what your should be aware of is the concept and that it is important to point out these various tools to your web site designer and ask your designer to include the tools in your site. Even though you are outsourcing the creation of your site and delegating the tasks, it is important that you still take on a distant hands-on approach. This means that you should not be involved in every detail of the creation process or micromanage the task but allow the person you have hired to design your site to do the job without interference from you. On the other hand, you should be keeping up to date with the designer about the different tools that you discover and desire to have on the site. You could send the designer a daily e-mail alert about to the different tools that you have found online which could help with your web site. You could e-mail suggestions or periodically meet with the designer to discuss how it is progressing and different ideas about what you want to have included in your site. You still have to allow the designer to use his or her own expertise to design the site. Many people start out by delegating but then become so involved in the actual task that the designer who really knows how to design the sites ends up more or less "surrendering" and just listening to the owner's advice and ignoring their own expert ideas. What happens is that many good creative ideas generated by the professionals end up going to waste because the designer cannot use them. On the other hand, you can be proactive in suggesting ideas to the web site designer by showing him the online tools you like and by outlining a concrete strategy to follow in designing the site. This is fine, but once you make the suggestions you allow the designer to create his or her own interpretation of your ideas using their skills. Once the site is complete and you review it then together you can make adjustments. Always allow the designer to use his or her own professional skills to complete the task that you have given to them.

Having a site designer work on your site is great because it helps you with networking. By this, I mean that the site designer can put you in touch with some of his other clients and you can discuss with the clients what has worked for them in site design and in marketing the sites, how they deliver products or services to consumers, and which are the best advertising venues. There are many ideas and strategies that you can take by having the ability to direct not only the clients of the site designer but also the designer himself. Let us say that you get into a conversation with the designer and you tell them that you need to advertise your site and you would like to hear some of his suggestions. He may tell you "I have five clients and out of them three clients advertise on this specific web site which is very successful at producing results." Then you can apply that information to your own web site by including information in your business plan. When the site is ready and you want to start advertising, you can start the advertising using that information. You would not know that information without having a professional web designer with whom to discuss the business ideas. So having a designer is great because they will also act as a free consultant for you. The advice they give you is free because they have gathered it by doing business online and doing work for other people who have online businesses.

Having a site designer is also good because that person's active involvement in web design allows them to be continuously abreast of developments in the online world. If the designer comes across a tool that can help your site attract more customers or turn more visitors into customers then the designer can let you know. If they come across a great advertising tool, they can also tell you about it. If the web site designer is aware of a new opportunity in the online world then they will alert you to the opportunity and you can discuss it together and see how you can take advantage of it to make money. The reason that site designers have an incentive to alert you to this opportunity is because they know that if you do go ahead and decide to pursue the opportunity they will be the one who is responsible for helping you to create a site or online presence to take advantage of it. This is a win-win situation for both you and the web site designer.

Even with a web site like eBay.com, which is a tremendous company, and as an online business, the success factor is its basic flea market approach as opposed to the actual design of its site. However, the site is still designed by professionals and is also maintained by them as well. One could make a mistake by saying, "Look, since eBay.com has such a tremendous concept in regards to attracting customers and making money, then maybe the actual design of the site and its maintenance are not important." This person would conclude from the information that someone who is auctioning products on eBay.com or buying products there is not that concerned with the look and appearance of the site. This would be a mistaken thought because people do enjoy shopping in an environment that makes them feel comfortable and is attractive to them whether it is in an offline presence or online presence. The managers of eBay.com are aware of this so they have professional designers who are continuously working on the design or maintenance of the web site. The same is true for the Amazon.com or the Yahoo! search engine.

Yahoo! is an extremely competitive market that has to compete with Google.com, the AOL search engine and with other various search engines. In order for the managers of Yahoo! to keep the company ahead of the competition or even to keep up to par with the competition they have to continuously employ web site designers who can make changes and maintain the site to make their search engine the most friendly site for visitors and to include any of the latest developments that are being used by the competition.

Who else uses site designers? Anyone from small companies such as movie companies and small shopping centers, to Blockbuster, Kmart, Wal-Mart, Macy's, and JC Penney. Most department stores have websites to provide information for their customers and to keep them updated on sales. If the sites were not professionally designed, the customers might get the wrong impression and their perception of the store might change causing them to shop elsewhere. Now if this is true for all of these major stores, then think about how much more important it is for a smaller operation like the start up operation that you may decide to launch. If a small store wants to be able to compete with a large national discount chain, then the small 99-Cents store must portray and market itself in every possible way to stand out from its competition and to be able to create an impression that will attract customers who would otherwise shop at the national discount chain.

What could this small 99-Cents store do? It could have a web site designer create a professional web site and list a few featured items arriving at the store each day. There could be a featured daily sale or a coupon that customers could print from the web site for presenting at the store to receive a free gift with their purchases. By the 99-Cents store having a professional web site with special promotions, it will be able to attract visitors to its actual retail location. A web site should also have an e-commerce component so that customers can buy their merchandise directly from the site. If you are a customer in a rural area then you may appreciate being able to order 99-cent items from the store even if it is located on the other side of the country. You might not order just two or three items but might order 20 or 30 items because of the great price offered and the quality of goods from the store. You will probably continue to order as long as the site is professional in appearance portraying credibility and assuring quality and customer satisfaction. If all of these factors are met, then you will feel inclined to order from the web site regardless of how small the actual retail store.

There are many online entrepreneurs who have closed down their retail locations after having web sites developed for them. These web sites were so successful and professional looking in giving such a good impression that these entrepreneurs no longer needed a retail location. I know of an eBay.com entrepreneur who was also an online vendor and closed her children's clothing store to devote her time and expertise completely to selling online through auctions and web sites because the online venture grew larger and faster than the retail business. In order for this to take place, the entrepreneur needs to have a web site that is going to deliver its message to customers coming across in such a strong way that those customers will feel as if their best option is to buy online. After all, if they are being offered such a good deal by this online retailer why should they shop elsewhere and why should they spend their time shopping offline.

How should choose a professional web designer? You can search online at sites including eBay.com, Creativemoonlighter.com and many other sites where you can post a project and then people bid on your project contacting you for your business. You can search for designers on Google.com, AOL.com, Yahoo!.com, national newspapers such as the New York Times, Wallstreet Journal or any local newspaper or trade journal. I see site designers advertising in the Daily News or the New York Post and I am sure that this is true for any town in the United States. As long as there is a demand for web sites there will be people advertising their skills. Remember, just because someone has a flashy advertisement it does not mean that their services are expensive. It could just be that they are doing a very good job of marketing themselves and are portraying themselves positively.

They either have created a fancy ad themselves or have saved their resources in order to advertise in a more expensive publication. Their services however, may be very affordable and after all, everything is negotiable. Even if they have an initial fee that is too expensive for you, either work on reducing the fee or discuss with them what added value services they can include in the price so that you will receive more for your money. If their fee range begins at $300-$500 for designing a site, you could negotiate for a reduced fee of a hundred dollars less or you could present them with the option of providing an additional service in exchange for your payment.

Among the services you can negotiate to receive is advice on where to advertise, banner ad creation, e-zine creation meaning an online newsletter, design advertisements to use online, help develop an online business strategy, consulting with you on various online business issues like helping to locate some one to do payment processing. There are many services that the web site designer can offer and which you can also offer him or her as benefits of doing business with you. You could tell the designer that in exchange for a reduction of the fee you will allow the designer to advertise their services on your web site. Not only that, but that you will actively advertise their services along with your products and services as long as you receive a sizeable discount from your fee. Most designers will agree to this because they would rather give up a portion of their profits today in order to capture more profits over the long term, just as you are willing to earn a smaller profit on your initial order if you can capture future profits that come from future orders from your customers. Many variations exist in negotiation techniques that you can use but the most important point is that at the end of the day, you have a professional web site designer creating and maintaining your site.

Chapter Ten

Having customers visit your web site takes skill and strong strategies that must be implemented correctly. Getting customers to stay on your site is another matter. Having customers stay on your site is even more important than getting them to visit the site to begin initially. I would rather have 100 customers come to my site and stay there as opposed to having 1, 000 customers briefly visit and then leave for another online destination. Studies have found that the longer a customer stays on your site, the more chance there is that the visitor will make a purchase from your site, enter their contact information, leave a message, or inquire about a product or service that you are offering.

Many web site research firms refer to this as the "stickiness factor" of a web site. In other words, how long will a customer stay at your site? Remember, the longer they stay, the more chance exists that they will interact with your site. Getting the customer to return to your site is equally important. Studies have found that the average customer must visit a site roughly seven times before they will purchase an order from you. This does not mean that in order for you to make money, all of your visitors must visit your site seven times. What this actually means is that for every 100 visitors that come to the site, if you have a good sales offering, good ad content and good copy writing on the site as well as good photographs then you are conveying a strong online presence and you could have 1% initial conversion rate. This means that 1% of your customers will make a purchase the first time they visit your site. The next time those customers return, out of those 99 customers who come back again 1% may make a purchase. If any given visitor returns to your site seven times, then those visitors will be a likely purchaser for you. At that time the conversion ratio from that visitor who has returned to your site seven times might be as high as 50%. This is because the actual sale is almost assured that this customer has a reason for visiting your site and enjoys it. The more that this customer is exposed to your site, even if he does not make a purchase, he will definitely leave his customer information or will interact with the site in some manner.

How do you get a customer to not only come to your site, stay on your site for an extended period of time and then give your customer a reason to return in the future? The way that you do that is by offering content on the site that is useful and practical for your intended audience. If you have a web site that is selling bicycles online, then your intended audience is either people who enjoy bicycle riding for the fun of it or your intended audience might be professional bikers who compete in races or could be individuals who are looking to get into shape and lose weight and they could be considering riding a bicycle as the exercise that will enable them to get to the fitness level that they desire.

You first need to determine the audience for which you are aiming. If you decide that you are aiming for the professional biker audience, then you need to tailor your information to that audience. In this case, you should have articles on your site dealing with how to become a professional bike rider, how to develop skills and stamina, where to find the best competitions, where to find tracks for training, where to find beautiful bicycle paths for riding an extended period of time, how cyclists can protect themselves from accidents, and which foods and drinks are best for replenishing energy while riding? By providing these articles that deal with the issues concerning your intended market, those visitors will be interested in what your site has to offer. Even if these visitors do not initially decide to purchase a bicycle from your site, they will stay on your site to read the articles and the information that is being offered to them on your web site.

An effective means by which you can capture their attention even more is by having different pages with different categories of articles. You could have one category of articles that deals with riding your bike in hot weather, another category regarding cold weather riding, and a different category dealing with clothing riding for extended riding. Another category could deal with accident prevention while another could offer articles about recovery from accidents. Safety is a very relevant category to address to an audience interested in bicycles.

You can further break down the categories into those dealing specifically with women or men and then children. Have categories that deal only with senior citizens. As your target audience comes to your site, give them enough reasons to continue staying there. Have articles that will be continued the following day or the following week. This way you give your visitor an incentive to return to your site.

For instance, let's say that you are selling a book that teaches how to invest in international securities. When an individual visits your site and he starts by reading your articles on the best countries in which to invest. Your first article covers China, while your second article will cover France. The visitor who has read the first article on China is very impressed with the information that you have provided so now he wants to know why you feel that people should invest in France. At that point, you should write on your web site that the article will be posted next week. This way the visitor who just read the article will have to return to your site in order to be able to read the second article. If you keep this type of a formula in place where the visitor has to keep returning on a weekly basis each time they return, you are moving towards the goal of having your visitor at your site seven times. The more times visitors return to the site, the more chances there are that they will purchase what you are offering. In the case of the investment course book, if this visitor reads five to seven articles then that visitor has returned to your site seven times on average. He has had to stay on your site for ten-twenty minutes because he has been reading all of the articles on your site. Consider what a good chance there is that by the 7th time that visitor will be so convinced by the value of your information that they will buy what you are offering.

The point of this exercise is to capture the attention of visitors. Have the visitors not only focus on your site but also stay on your site and perceive your site as a valuable tool for receiving the information that interests them. When they realize the value of your information, they will also realize that the products and services that you offer must also be of equal value. The same takes place when you sell your investment course book from your web site and you offer articles on investing. What ends up happening is if the visitor to your site is so impressed by your style of writing and the information that you are providing, then they will conclude that the information available through the book you are selling must be written in a professional manner and also must give an equal amount of useful and practical investment information.

Whether you are selling bicycles online or selling an investment course book online, the key is in being able to have an offering on your site that will capture the attention of visitors and cause them to return to your web site. Another technique you should implement a message board. We will discuss message boards in detail later but one of the benefits of a message board is that people will return to the site to read of other people's experiences daily on the subject that you are covering in your web site. They will want to share their comments and will post questions and return to the site to see the answers that are posted in reply to their questions. As you can see, a message board encourages visitors to return to websites.

You can allow your visitors to receive a subscription from your site regarding information for which they are looking. When they come to your site, they can subscribe to the information and as they receive your newsletter, they will be reminded of your site and return periodically. The best tool for having visitors return to your site is daily-changing information through your site. This way, you are assured that if the visitors are interested in what you are offering, and most likely they are interested or they would not have visited in the first place, then by offering information you will be giving your visitors a reason to return continuously to your site.

Remember, your goal is not just to have visitors arrive at your site for the first time, but to have them continue returning to your site as many times as possible. At some point when they have seen your sales message a number of time and the credibility of your site has been established, they will perceive your offering as having a high level of value. They then will become customers of your site and at the minimum, give you their personal information so that you can continue to contact them and send your offerings to them. I know of many successful web sites that even though they have a very low level of traffic and receive a low level of visitors, but because those visitors are loyal visitors who continuously return to the site, they become acclimated to them and end up interacting with the site and doing business there.

I remember seeing a web site that was devoted to selling a magic course. The magic course was aimed at professional magicians who put on shows, look for bookings and want to expand their careers. Most magicians who do this as a profession might not be aware of this course and even if they were aware of the course might already have their own ideas, which they follow and might not be open to trying out new ideas. This web site that sells the magic course for professionals does very well because even though it is serving a small niche market its visitors continuously return to the site to see what advice and tips are posted on the site because they can use this information. If they want even more advice and information, they order the magic course because they realize that if the advice and tips they are receiving are good then the actual course must be even better.

Remember, in order to attract customers to your web site and to turn the customers into interactive customers who will continuously buy from you, always give them a reason to come to your site, stay on your site and to return as well.

Chapter Eleven

When running an online business it is very important that you have a system to capture leads from your customers. These leads are the leads that will actually turn your visitors into customers. In business, these leads are referred to as sales leads. They are the names and contact information of perspective customers who by contacting you will have the opportunity to turn into customers. Having sales leads while running an online business is very important since unlike in an offline business, there is no guarantee that you will ever see these customers again or that these customers will ever see your business again. See, one advantage that a retail store has over an online retail site is that its perspective customers will see the retail store numerous times because every time they drive by they will see the store. On the other hand, a perspective customer from an online retail store might only visit the web site once and then either forget about the web site or simply never go back to the web site because the site did not have anything that interested the customer at the time the customer visited.

If you can capture the contact information of that customer then you can remind them of your site either by sending the customer e-mail offerings or contacting the customer by phone or having other types of advertisements tailor made for the customer that would turn your customer into a purchaser at your online retail store. As you see, it is very important to capture sales leads for your online business whether your business is a business-to-business site or it is a consumer-to-business site selling directly to consumers. If you go online and visit any professional e-commerce site, you will see that they put a lot of effort into capturing your e-mail address and your contact information because they realize that you may never visit their site again and they want the opportunity to be able to contact you and extend their offers to you. By being able to extend those offers to you in the future, they will have another opportunity to receive business from you.

The question now becomes "How do you capture your customer's contact information?"

The basic method is by simply asking your visitors for their e-mail addresses, their names, addresses, phone numbers, mailing addresses. A certain percentage of visitors may leave this information if they are interested in what your site is offering. Let's say that you run into a situation where they are simply not interested in what you are offering at the time or they are interested but have other things on their mind. Unless you give them an incentive to leave their contact information, they will not take the time to provide you with a way to contact them in the future.

Let's say that someone hears of a great web site that is offering a specialized basketball sneaker that he or she would be interested in buying. They go to the site and see that the sneaker is actually sold out that week, so they leave the site and look for another outlet to buy the sneaker. They might not return to the site a week later to check and see if the sneaker is available because in that time, they may have forgotten about the site, lost the address or at worst they may be already shopping retail locations to buy the sneaker. What can you do? You need to find a method for capturing a customer's contact information so that you can alert them as soon as the sneaker comes back into stock. This way even if the customer forgot about your site, you are reminding them about the site. If they are already shopping offline you could capture their attention and bring them back to your site.

So, how do you capture this contact information? Well, the best way to do it is to give your customers an incentive for providing their information to you. Anytime that you can put in something for a potential customer, meaning that giving you their information is in their best interest, they will gladly provide their information. If you pay your customers for their contact information, they will happy to give it to you just to make money. Since that is not economically feasible in most situations, you will have to find another technique for giving customers a strong benefit that will make them willing to give you the information. How can you accomplish this? You can offer special discounts in exchange for the information. If you have a site that sells sneakers, and there are many successful sites that devote themselves to selling shoes and sneakers, you can offer a 10% discount coupon, which will be e-mailed to them in exchange for their providing the contact information to you. This way even if they are not interested at the time in ordering a pair of sneakers from you, or if they are not certain whether they want to order online, they will still want to take advantage the opportunity to receive a 10% discount so they will give you the information. Once they receive that 10% discount they may decide to buy or even if they're not interested you will have their contact information so you can follow up by contacting them enough times to encourage them to come to your site. Remember if they visit your site an average of seven times, that customer will become a consumer and will buy from your site so it is very important that you find a way to capture your customer's information.

What is another way to capture that information? You can set up an information package on your site such a free e-book which is a downloadable book containing information aimed at your target audience. The way to do this is to offer a link with a small paragraph underneath it explaining that by clicking on the link customers will receive a complete book dealing with the subject in which they are interested.

If your web site deals with music and your focus is in classical music, then you can have an e-book devoted to teaching people about various classical composers. It will contain information that exposes them to new types of classical music of which they may not have been aware in the past. The first of two benefits from this is that when the customers read the information they will be excited about the classical music and it might turn them into buying customers. Secondly, in exchange for receiving the e-book they will have to give their contact information.

You can use the contact information as sales leads and contact the customers in order to encourage them to buy from you. Remember, your goal is to always offer something free to your customers in exchange for their contact information. Give the customer something for free that will either fulfill a need of theirs or the benefit for which they are looking motivating them to give you that information. When you ask for the information, make sure to also convey the message that you will not be sharing their information with any other parties, that you will respect their privacy and that you will never send them spam or bombard their e-mail boxes. Also, advise that you will only be contacting them on a periodic basis so that the customer need not be concerned with receiving an excessive amount of advertising from you. This way they know that you respect their privacy and that you will only use the information to deliver sales opportunities that they can appreciate. Also, when you explain to the customers why you want the information, be straightforward. Tell your customer that this is the best way for you to keep in touch with them and to alert them to special opportunities and offers that are available to them. The customer will understand that you want the opportunity to sell to them but they will also appreciate the fact that they will be receiving special information on special sales that will be taking place. If you want to insure that your customer does give you the information, also let them know that you will be sending them practical information that is applicable to them that they can use actively in their personal lives or their businesses.

You see the customer who has come to your site, has come there for a reason. Ask yourself what that reason is and what they are looking to gain by coming to your site. If you can offer that benefit to the customers and you can offer that same benefit on a continual basis, then they will give you the contact information.

Let's say that you have a site concerning fishing. Your customers come to your site looking to buy fishing supplies. The first thing that you know is that they enjoy fishing. Now you have to find at whether they enjoy it as a hobby, whether they teach fishing, whether it is possible that they work at a tourist location taking people out on fishing trips, or whether perhaps they fish as a profession. You will have to decide which niche that you are targeting. Once you make this decision, you also determine why your customers are coming to your site. Ask them for their contact information and let them know that you will be sending them information along with special offers and special sales. You can tell them that they will also be receiving special information that they can use when they are fishing. Regardless of why they are fishing, make sure that you are sending information that is targeted to that need and which delivers the benefit for which they are looking. If a customer comes to your site and sees that he can receive a ready supply of valuable information from which he could benefit from then he will have no problem giving you his contact information as long as he knows that you will respect their privacy and will never abuse the information or share it with outside parties. If you do want to use the contact information by either renting it or selling it to third parties you may do so as long as you alert your customers ahead of time advising them that if they ever receive any e-mail which they no longer want to receive that you can and will immediately remove them from your list. In any event, make sure your customers know that if at any point in the future after giving you the information they decide that they no longer want to be contacted they can send you an e-mail and you will delete their information and send no future correspondence . This way, they are assured that they do not have to be concerned at all. They will know that their privacy is protected and that they can stop receiving communications from you at any point. On the upside, they will be receiving great offers for good sales and special prices.

Chapter Twelve

Now that we have established the need to keep track of your sales leads, we will discuss the next step. It is very important to have an e-mail list that specifically collects all of the e-mail addresses of prospective customers. By that I mean that besides having a data base consisting of all your prospects who have ever expressed any interest in your web site, your products, your information or any other contacts, you should have an e-mail list of these prospects which you can use to send out e-mail whenever you want. There are services that will allow you to send out an e-mail to your list anytime you choose. You can hire a service that will charge you to send out a certain amount of mail on a daily, weekly, monthly or yearly basis. You can also send them out directly from your own computer. It is important that when you have this list of e-mail prospects it will be very easy to send out e-mail periodically to remind prospects about offers and sales opportunities that you have on your web site. If you do not have a well defined list then you will lose prospects because remember it takes up to seven times of a prospect's coming to your site to produce the likely result of that prospect becoming a customer. By sending this e-mail promotion to your prospects, you will be able to reach and remind a number of people about your products and services. You will then be able to get them to become customers of your site.

What should be enclosed in the e-mails that you send? Well for starters, you do not want to just send them a sales offer or a special discount on a product or service that you offer as they will see this merely as an advertisement. Even if they look at the e-mail, they will delete it and all it has amounted to is an advertisement that they will not read. Instead, you want to send e-mail that contains information that they will be excited to receive. You want them to look forward to receiving your e-mail so that they get accustomed to receiving quality information from you that they can use. Each time they see a letter in their e-mail box originating from you they will open it and read it to gain access to the valuable information you provide.

What you should do is follow two approaches. One approach that I will discuss first is having the sales that you are offering your prospects at the head of the article since they will find an article very useful. You are writing information that could help them in the practical sense that is related to your web site, and it must be related, since the only reason you have their e-mail address is that they have expressed an interest in your site. Why send them an e-mail on a different topic about which you do not necessarily know they are interested in reading.

After they read the information, they can then see that you have a special offer related to the products and services in which they are interested. This way if they are interested in what you are offering they will follow the link and go to your site to see view the sale and the product that you are offering and read more about it. What you can do instead of putting the link at the bottom of the e-mail you should make it a clickable HTML link or an active link so that when they click on the link they are immediately taken to your site requiring a minimum amount of effort on their part. The less effort required on their part, the better your chances that they will go to your site and investigate your offering.

Another option for including a sales offer in your e-mail is to make it a part of the article you are featuring. As you discuss information that is pertinent to your prospects' interests, include your offer in a way relates it to what you are discussing. Let's say for example that you have a web site that specializes in educational material geared towards high school teachers. The educational material that you sell will help high school teachers teach the subjects to their students. You now have that e-mail list consisting of prospects or teachers who teach at the high school level and have expressed an interest in what you are offering. You may want to send them an e-mail containing an article on the best way to explain Astronomy to 9th graders who do not have a background in science. You could write a very informative article, which the teachers find very interesting, and they will want to read in its entirety. As you write that article if you have a book on your web site that instructs teachers how to teach Astronomy in very basic terms then you can use examples from the book that you sell. Therefore, instead of just pitching the book to the teachers in your e-mail article once or twice you can reference examples from the book that is available on your site. The curiosity of these teachers is peaked because they have enjoyed reading the tips offered by the article. If they want to know more about this book, they will then visit your site to learn more about it. If they are then convinced that the book can really help them teach Astronomy to their students then they will purchase the book from your site.

Another example is that you have a web site that sells teddy bears and you have a list of 200 prospects who have expressed an interest in your teddy bears. These prospects already like teddy bears that have to do with different professions. They like to buy doctor teddy bears, police officer teddy bears, dentist teddy bears, fire-fighter teddy bears or whichever profession they are geared towards or perhaps they are people who like to buy gifts for those professionals. So now, let's say that you have sent out an article on teddy bears, which will be a very interesting article on when they were first made, who made the first teddy bear, what the most favorite teddy bears are in a certain country and at a certain time in history. When you write that article, you could use examples from the teddy bears that you sell. You can write an article saying how that in the early 1900's in Spain the most popular teddy bear was the soldier teddy bear because Spain was involved in a war or Spain had just won a war at that time. You could then say that you happen to carry this teddy bear at your site, or in order to avoid portraying that the e-mail has a sales pitch; you could write that a picture of this famous bear is available at your site by following a link that you provide. Then they could click on the link and see the teddy bear. The chances are that they will click on the link out of curiosity because they will want to see the teddy bear that is being discussed in the article. Once they look at the teddy bear on your site, they will then obviously have the opportunity to buy the teddy bear. The key is not to make your approach direct sales pitch since these people are only prospects. They have not yet bought anything from you and have not yet actually expressed an interest in buying from you. You have to continue to ferment their curiosity the point where they will make a purchase. Remember, the best way to capture a prospect's attention and turn a prospect into a customer is by sending them an e-mail that contains practical information or information that they find enjoyable and can use such as example products or services that you offer thus directing their attention to your site. In addition, you must have pictures or more information related to the article on your site. Meaning, with the teddy bear example, you let people know in your e-mail that if they want to see pictures of this famous teddy bear, they should click on the HTML link to arrive on your site.

On the other hand, let's say you are writing an article on the best types of vitamins that people should take to prevent hair loss. Now you do not want to just attempt selling the vitamins to prevent hair loss directly through your e-mail newsletter because then people will see it as a sales pitch and as just another hair loss product but if they are only prospects and did not buy anything in the first place, the chances are they will simply delete your e-mail. As an alternative, if you discuss the benefits of taking certain types of vitamins to prevent hair loss and then you conclude the article by stating that if people want to read more information on what vitamins that they can take to prevent hair loss, they should visit your site. You put the link at the bottom of the e-mail and they click on it because they are interested in learning more about the vitamins that they should be taking for hair loss. Then they arrive at your web site offering vitamins and relevant information aimed at that niche encouraging them to eventually buy the vitamins. This takes place because your prospect will go to your web site to read more about the vitamins you are offering and if they read enough to convince them that the vitamins really do work and it is to their benefit to take the vitamins for themselves or someone else who, then they will buy them from you because they are already at your site.

If you look at the web site of GNC or any other health or nutrition minded company you will notice that they devote a lot of time and space not just to push-ing their products and not just selling the products that they carry but they also to explaining the benefits of the different products that they carry. The reason is because they know that if they can convince you of the need to take their prod-ucts or if they can convince you of the benefits of purchasing from them, once you make the decision to take those vitamins, the most logical place for you to buy them is at their site because you were already there when you made the deci-sion. This is not to say that I recommend someone should take a supplement but what I do recommend is that you should mimic their marketing strategies where they spend time with the consumer convincing them of the benefit of their prod-ucts or services and then allow the customer to make the next decision by pur-chasing the products or services from their web site.

If you look up an e-health magazine or any workout magazine, you will notice that they use the same strategy. If you look at "Muscle and Fitness" or any publi-cation that caters to the body-building market you will notice that all of them are actually advertisements which are written in efforts of trying to sell a nutritional supplement. You will notice that the majority of the article is not devoted towards actually selling the supplements. The article is devoted to convincing people of their need regarding taking that nutritional supplement and it is also looking to convince people of the benefits that they can derive from taking that nutritional supplement. The article ends by saying that the nutritional supplement that this company is offering is the best and can deliver the results for which these people are now looking and the benefits that those people would like to receive.

You will need to use the same strategy with your e-mail campaign when it goes out to your sales prospects. They need to be alerted to the fact that they have a need for what you offer. You need to be able to showcase the benefits of what you are offering and then you need to conclude by directing them towards making a purchase from your site for the products or services.

The last thing that you want to do with the e-mail prospect list is simply convince them that they have a need for your products or services and then direct them towards your site. You always want to help people make a decision by at some point guiding them and directing them towards your web site. Remember, do not end off your article by telling people that "Now you can go to my web site and purchase my merchandise at a 10% discount if you act now." Instead, end your e-mail by saying something like "If you visit my site you will be able to gain more of an insight into some of the tremendous additional benefits that you can receive by using my products or services." Remember to make it sound realistic and as if the customers could really gain if they act now. Remember, always stay away from the fly-by-night image. This image would urge people that by not acting now they will miss your offer. You may want to put an expiration date on your offer or a limit to put a sense of urgency in people but don't try to convince people that if they don't act now they will never be able to purchase what you are offering again. Most people know that this is not the case and after all, you want to be able to portray a long-term business presence to your online customers and perspective customers.

Chapter Thirteen

Besides compiling an e-mail list consisting of your prospects you will also want to have separate e-mail lists consisting of the e-mail address of all of your customers. The reason that you need to have two separate lists is that the way that you will market to people who have already purchased from you will be different that the way that you market to people who have never purchased from you. The reason is that people who have already purchased from you feel that they have a relationship with you and rightfully feel that they are entitled to special services and discounts because they have the relationship with you. They do not need to be convinced of the benefits of the products or services and that you offer. What they need is a constant flow of communication to remind them of the products or services that you offer and to keep them up to date when you have special promotions and offers. On the other hand, your prospective customers are people who do not have a relationship with you and you are using the e-mail list to build a relationship with them.

So now, let's address the need for building an e-mail listing consisting of your customers. For starters, the need to have a customer e-mail list is because you do want to stay in touch with all of your customers. By staying in touch with all of your customers, you will be able to gain more sales because if you do not stay in touch with your customers then they will soon forget about your products or services. No matter how much they enjoy the products or services that you are able to deliver, they will soon forget about them because they have other things on their mind and other activities that they deal with in their life. Even if they do need your product or service, again if they do not have your web site name in their mind they could go somewhere else to buy their product or service. I have been involved in many situations where a customer of mine bought something from another source simply because the customer was not aware that I carried that product or service or the customer was in the situation where they did not think to buy from me only because my business was not on his mind.

Donny Lowy • 75

Now in order for you to avoid that situation you want to be constantly communicating with your customers. You need to remind them of all of the products or services that you offer. In my own wholesale business while I primarily wholesale socks, whether they are adult socks or children's socks I also wholesale many other items including undershirts, tee shirts, and different types of closeouts. My customers know me for socks. They may also know me for tee shirts. Many of my customers may not realize that I also deal with closeouts. The reason why I continuously want to e-mail my customers is to alert them to the fact that I have other types of products besides my primary products. The reason that I need to do this is that I do not when one of my customers will be looking for a closeout that I may be carrying. If I don't alert all of my customers to the products or services that I offer then my customers might not offer anything to me and may not even be aware that I have what they are looking for.

For instance, I had a closeout deal where I was able to purchase a large number of comic books at a very good price. I had to go ahead and alert all of my customers and let them know that I was carrying the comic books because some of my customers, while they primarily buy socks from me, they have discount stores or 99 cent stores that can make money if they stock comic books. Therefore, I let customers know and gave them the option to buy comic books from me. The same takes place with other closeouts that I bought such as greeting cards. I bought greeting cards and alerted my customers to the fact that I carried greeting cards and I marketed them until I found the owner of a 99-Cent store who bought all of the cards from me. As you can see, by constantly marketing and always staying in touch with your customers you can update them to new products and services and alert them to any changes that you have. When I have a special that I want to move out since I am closing the books for the month or because I want the space for another order with my suppliers, I will send out special offerings to my customers to let them know that if they buy now I will give them a special discount as opposed to when they normally buy. The reason I do this is so that I can move merchandise when I need to bring in or am bringing in other merchandise. You will want to have the same strategy with your web site.

If your web site is selling toys online then you need continuously to update your customers about all of the toys that you carry. This way your customers will be aware that you do not just carry the toy that they want but you also carry other toys. In addition, you should send out an e-mail alerting them to any special sales that you may be having. If any of your customers may not be specifically interested in a given toy that you are selling at a certain time or they are not currently in the market for that toy but they see that you are having a special sale they may buy it anyway and set it aside for a special occasion when they can use it as a gift. They may buy the toy even if they are not interested in it but because it is being offered at a very good price and they may become interested. By having the e-mail list by which you can contact all of your customers and continuously alert them to the new offerings that you have, you will be able to keep them as customers for a long time and increase sales by encouraging your customers to buy from you more often. The more they can see your company's products and services the more opportunities that they will to buy your products or services.

Now when you actually send out your e-mail to customers, you want to also include information that is pertinent to the product. Only give them useful information so that they will also look forward to reading your e-mails. If your customers feel that all your e-mails are just advertisement, even if they are concerning what you are offering, they may soon delete your e-mails and stop reading them all together. Make sure that what you are sending is useful to them and applicable to them.

Considering the web site that sells toys, you may want to send interesting articles on the latest toys that are available on the market and you may want to add articles about why certain toys are so popular and add something to show the most popular toys of the current season. You can end the e-mail with a direct link to your site where there are more pictures of the toys or read more about them. If they are interested then they can make a decision to purchase. You do not want to actually advertise the sale in your e-mail because you want to elicit an interest in the products or services that you are selling, lead the customer to the site and then let the site do the selling. Your site will have a better chance of selling the toy than an e-mail can is because there is only so much information that you can enclose in an e-mail.

Let's say that you have a web site that sells musical instruments and you write a very interesting article regarding the development of the trumpet over the years and people find the article very interesting and they are curious, want to read more, and go to visit your site. After they have read up on the trumpet on your site and they looked at all of the pictures you have posted, they may decide that they do not want to buy a trumpet. Once they are at your site and they browse through the rest of the site, they may see a great offer on a flute and may be interested in the flute. The key is that once you bring the visitors to your site, then the visitor naturally, if they are interested in what you are offering, will browse your web site. This is what retail stores do when they advertise loss leaders. A loss leader is a product or service that is advertised at a price reflecting a loss. The hope is that when the customer comes in to buy the loss leader he or she will end up buying other products and services that will earn a profit.

Online retailers do this by advertising a product at an extremely low price and the customer then goes to the web site and purchases that product the site is counting on the fact that the customer will not only purchase that product but will also purchase accessories that are related to that product. The company can make money not only on the loss leader product but it will make a profit on the accessories that it is selling.

The key is to always find ways to bring customers to your site or offline store by sending out e-mails to remind them of your site and what it offers, giving them a reason to come to the site. This way you will be able to keep your customers returning and then buying.

In all of your e-mails, whether sent to your prospect list or to your customer list, you should always a forward option so that your e-mail can be forwarded to other people who might be interested. This allows you to simply ask people to forward your e-mail to anyone else who might be interested in your products or services. You could also have a link that allows people to send you an e-mail with a friend's address or contact information for someone else who would enjoy learning more about your subject.

If you are sending out a letter to those who have purchased from your web site, then have a link stating that if you know of anyone else who would be interested in learning about the pet supplies and special offers that you have, please click here. When they click on the link, another e-mail opens with your address in the "send to" area. Then all they need to do is type the e-mail address of the new contact they are supplying for you in the "subject" area. You will receive an e-mail from a designated address of yours letting you know right away why you are receiving an e-mail with someone's address in the subject line. You then take that address and you add it to your prospect list and send an e-mail to that person with an introductory paragraph explaining how you received their address and why you are sending them information. Always give them an "opt out option" but at the same time, give them a strong reason as to why they should continue to subscribe to your newsletter and how it is in their benefit to receive e-mails from you. By using this strategy, you will be able to gain customers and prospects from the e-mails that you send out currently to your prospects and customers.

Think about also what could be better than having a sales lead or having a customer referred to you by someone who has already used your products or services. After all, from whom would you buy? Would you buy your life insurance from an agent you do not know or would you prefer to buy from an agent who also has a professional-looking web site and has actually done business writing a policy for a close relative or business associate of yours? I think that you can agree with me that you would rather buy insurance from the agent who has already dealt with someone that you know. You would also be more than willing to meet with that person as long as someone who had already used that person's service referred you to that person. Imagine that you are contacted by that life insurance agent's client and are hearing, "Look, this is a great person with whom you should do business." When you hear from that agent, you will at least be interested because an acquaintance or relative will have referred you.

The same is true with online businesses. You want to offer the option for people to refer business associates and friends to your web site because those referrals will be extremely important and strong because the people who are doing the referrals are those who have a relationship with the person being referred. The person being referred will check out your web site and will check out your products or services because they trust the judgment of the person who has referred them to you. If anything, they are curious to see why the person whom they know is referring them to you and at a basic level, they will give you a chance. The key is to continuously send e-mails to your prospects and customers to build a relationship with them and to allow it to develop with other people whom they have in their sphere of influence. If you do this, not only will you be building a strong relationship but will also be building a relationship with potential customers who are outside of your sphere of influence. You will no longer have to rely completely on advertising to draw customers in because at some point you will want to be able to move away from spending money on advertising to basically running a campaign that does not require any advertising expense since you already have a large list of potential customers and a large list of actual customers.

Chapter Fourteen

In order to have a successful e-mail base for prospects and one for customers, you need to give them an option to include themselves on your list. Instead of you waiting to collect their e-mail addresses give them a way that they can put themselves onto your e-mail base. Now why would customers want to do this? Very simply, because they are interested in the products or services that you are offering on your web site. If your site caters toward the penny stock community or towards investors who want to buy penny stocks and they see that you have a newsletter providing instructional information on how to invest in penny stocks and how to find the best up and coming small companies, then they will want to subscribe to your e-mail newsletter so they can receive the information. If you do not give them the option to sign up at your web site then you are missing prospects. Not only will you not have a way to capture their e-mail addresses, but also they are people who are interested to begin with in receiving information from you. When you develop an online presence keep in mind that most people will simply go to your site and may leave your site because they have a lack of interest but only because they will not know how to contact people or at the time may not have an interest in contacting you to but would like to receive periodic information.

Let's look at the example with a site catering to penny stock investors. You sell, as I had a site once, that sells a course on penny stock investing. If you would like to know why I no longer have that site, it is that once I grew my business and I had already developed other businesses, I took my penny stock web site and sold the rights to the course. That individual then developed it into an even more successful online business, which enabled me to free my time to devote myself to other online businesses. I wanted to tell you this as a motivation as to why you should look at building an online business even if you do not plan to be committed on a long-term basis.

With my penny stock web site, there were many times that visitors came to the site and did not have a specific question for me. They read up on the course and half the time they really were not interested in the course but were interested in learning more about penny stocks. What I did was allow them to subscribe to my e-mail newsletter. They gave me their e-mail addresses and received information that they were interested in because they were investing in penny stocks and wanted to find more ways to invest in them. The first time they received the newsletter or the second or the third time, they might not have been interested in my course but maybe by the fourth or fifth time they received the newsletter they became interested in buying my course.

After the third or fourth e-mail, they already knew what I was talking about and therefore were willing to spend the $97.00 for my course. During the first few e-mails, they were reading the information and enjoying it but still trying a system that was being provided by another investment expert or perhaps even trying their own system. After numerous trial and error runs, they determined that their system or the system of another expert was not working for them. At that point, they would decide to go ahead and buy my course.

If I had not sent out my newsletters and I did not have them on my prospect list, when they were ready to try out another penny stock system, they would not have remembered my system and they would have tried someone else's system rather than mine since there would be no way to remind them of my web site. By reminding them about my system, I was giving them a reason to return time after time and then buy my course. Remember, my course was quite expensive at $97.00 while other similar investment courses were selling for $20.00 to $50.00. I needed to do whatever I could to insure that my customers saw my site and my course as many times as possible so that I would have a very good chance to sell it to them. I allowed them to register for my newsletter even if they did not express an interest in buying from me.

If you have a web site devoted to sports merchandise such as memorabilia then you also want to have a newsletter going out on all the latest trends in collecting sports memorabilia. Even if they are not interested in the items that you are selling or at that time, as long as you are getting this e-mail newsletter to them, they will keep your site in mind and continue to consider your products or services. Eventually they will find an article or a piece of information on your site that is interesting to them. There is no guarantee when this will happen. It could take from a week to six months down the line, but it does not matter to you as long as you have a system that is providing you with a steady stream of customers and prospects, you will be earning money.

How do you do this? You have a small box on you home page with an instruction paragraph underneath the box saying "If you would like to receive crucial information covering the subject matter that we are dealing with please enter your e-mail address and click enter." You will start receiving our extremely interesting and useful e-mail newsletter. The exact words that you use are up to you and you must make sure that the level of excitement matches the customer market that your are targeting.

A college audience would have a different type of language used than the language used in the senior citizen marketplace. The same would be true for a web site catering to Republicans or Democrats. The parties are interested in different issues and have different views to convince. When you want to convince them to subscribe to your newsletter, stress how your web site addresses those issues in which they are interested. Regardless of how you do it, make sure that you do have an option for people to join your mailing list.

While ideally, every prospect that comes to visit websites would become a customer, of course we would all love the fact that instead of having a conversion ratio of 1% or 2% or even 5% we all would love to have a conversion ratio of 100% or at the minimum of 50%. As we know, that in reality that does not take place. The majority of visitors who come to our sites for one reason or another will not make a purchase. We need to implement a system that will allow us to have one more opportunity to try to turn that visitor who is leaving the site into a customer.

So how do we do that? It is actually quite a difficult feat to accomplish because once someone is already leaving the site then he or she has clearly demonstrated that for one reason or another they are not interested in the product or service that you offering at that time. You need to determine first why someone would leave your site. Why would someone not be interested in the product or service that you are offering? Write down on paper the reasons that come to mind. What you could do is even ask people who do not have an interest in what you are offering, why they do not want to buy what you are offering. Make sure to also ask people who do have an interest in the area that you are doing business in because otherwise it will be like asking someone why he or she does not want to eat chocolate if he or she simply does not like junk food at all. You need to find a chocolate lover and ask them why they do not want to order your particular chocolate.

You want to ask a few people all of these reasons because many times people leave reasons on message boards that are not even a response to your product but a similar product or category in the same issue that is taking place on the market and is discouraging people from purchasing your products or services. You need to investigate these reasons and then make a list.

Write down 10-20 reasons why someone who comes to your site might at the end decide not to buy your products or services. One reason could be is that your price is too high. No matter what price you have there will always be those people who feel it is too expensive. Another reason could be that people feel they are not receiving enough for their money.

As you remember earlier, when we mentioned that you should always give a bonus away that has a high value perception attached to, the reason for giving the bonus is to answer this very problem. Another reason why someone may not buy from you is that they feel you may not have enough credibility, they may not know who you are and have never heard of you and do not feel comfortable doing business with you.

There are many other reasons why someone may not feel comfortable doing business with you and you need to list all of those reasons of which you can think. Try to come up with opposite reasons to counter these reasons and would satisfy someone who would otherwise not buy from you. Place each response next to the appropriate reason. As you go forward, you should be able to come up with more than a few reasons to counter every negative reason as to why someone is not buying from you.

You still have the same dilemma because even though you have all of your counter reasons in place you still have to convince those people who decided not to buy from you. The risk is that you do not want to alienate any potential customers and you do not want to convince people who were going to buy to then decide not to buy from you. How could this happen? If they read your reasons for buying from you, even though there are problems, then people may only focus on the problems. For instance, you do not want to put on your site, "Even though our price is high, the reason you should buy from us is because of so-and-so." Alternatively, "You may not know who we are but we are actually very reputable people." You will be putting into people's minds that there is a reason that maybe they should not be buying from you. Always stay positive when you are attempting to sell to prospects who have not decided if they want to buy from you or not. At the same time, you especially want to stay positive when you are dealing with customers who are returning to your site.

How do you deal with customers who have already made a decision not to buy from your site? Well, you should always have a link on your web site at the bottom that says, "If you have decided not to order at this time, please click here." When most people have decided not to order, they are ready to leave the site and you have nothing to lose by taking one last attempt to try to keep them on your web site. Even if people are now ready to leave the site, they may click on the link out of curiosity and see what you have to offer. Some people may even think that you are going to give away the product or service free because they decided not to buy. You need to have this link so that people have the opportunity to interact with site before they decide to leave it for good.

As we mentioned, the first thing is to have a link as described above. When they click on that link, they will be taken to a page where you will have one more opportunity to sell to them. On that page, you do not want to simply repeat the sales pitch that you made before because the sales pitch that you have was not enough for this customer. You need to have a different type of sales pitch now on this link. You know that the reason your customers did not buy from you is for the reasons on your list of reasons. If you did a good job of putting together an extensive list then you should have covered the majority of the reasons why they did not buy from you. The link page will be addressing all of those concerns, you will be addressing them in detail, and the actual sales pitch will be based on those reasons. You can also offer extra bonuses to your prospects on this page as you try to cover their concerns. If they felt that your price was too expensive, the first thing you do is to explain to them why it really is not too expensive and why it is reasonable. If they still feel they are not getting enough for their money, then be sure to offer extra bonuses so that they will definitely be getting enough value for their money. If your credibility is a concern then the way to address the concern is by writing about yourself and letting them know your background, who you are, why they should buy and what expertise goes into the selling of the products and services that your are offering.

The more information that you offer your customers, the better the chances are that they will respond to your products and services. All of this is true as long as the information that you are giving is in response to the need of the customer. In this situation, when a customer has decided not to order from you there is a certain need that should be addressed and that need is the desire for more information and assurances that they are making the right decision. So, remember that the key is to try first to find out why customers would not buy from you and then find ways to address those concerns. However, you should have those concerns on a separate section of your site as opposed to having them directly on the site where they could end up discouraging potential customers who may not have thought about those issues. This sales page should increase your conversion ratio because even if they do not initially buy from your site, as they leave and they go through this page you will have a final opportunity to turn them into paying customers.

Chapter Fifteen

Another strategy to insure that have gained the contact information for your customers prior to leaving your site or will help you sell to customers before they leave is what we call an exit pop-up. This is different from the pop-ups that you are used to seeing while browsing the web. A pop up is a web page that opens up when you go visit or surf on the Internet. It is a mini advertisement that could capture attention. The reason that a pop up is effective even though many people are annoyed by them and generally do not like them is that they get convey the message. The message appears in front of the consumer just when they are involved in a task that is associated with the message that the pop up is delivering.

For example, you are on a web site geared towards boxing gloves and as you leave the site, you see a pop up advertising of a special deal on boxing gloves. Even though the pop up ad is annoying since you want to leave and go to another site, it will definitely catch your attention since it is advertising merchandise in which you are interested. Not only that, the customer is receptive at the time because you were just reading a web site that pertains to boxing.

This same strategy is very effective when you are running your online business. When you are promoting or marketing your goods and services, you should consider using what I call an exit pop up. The pop up can either sell you products or services or it can ask for the contact information of your visitors. If it is geared towards capturing the e-mail address or other contact information of your visitors make sure that the ad offers a benefit that will encourage your visitors to leave that contact information. If the pop up is an attempt to sell merchandise before they leave the site, then also make sure that the ad will be delivering an offer that is too good to pass up on. You see, the offer that you are going to be giving has to be better than the offer that generally appears on your site but at the same time it has to have a lower price or people will complain. Let's say that I go visit a site that deals with wigs and I buy one of the wigs. As I leave the site, the wig for which I paid $19.95 is being sold through the pop up for only $14.95. I will be quite upset and not only will I ask for a refund, but I might not even buy the wig at the cheaper price because I will be unhappy with the entire process. So instead, what you should do is have a pop up offering on the same products or services that you have on the rest of your site for the same price. What you can do differently here is to give some extra bonuses or benefits along with the order. This way even if someone buys something and has not left the site and sees special bonuses being offered in the pop up they will not be upset because they can simply request the extra bonuses. You can even have bonuses that are not offered on the regular site and give those bonuses as a surprise to customers who have purchased your products or services. When they open the package with the products or services that they have purchased, they will be pleased.

When you have the pop up actually mention the gifts and bonuses someone who did not want to order will now be encouraged to order from you because they will see all of the extra benefits that they receive from ordering. The fundamental reason that you are giving away the fact that you will be giving the surprise bonuses in the pop up is as an extra incentive to convince a reluctant customer to actually buy from you. If you use the pop up feature constructively, it is not intrusive, and it appears immediately as soon as someone leaves the site it can be a great marketing tool.

There is software available on the market that will take you through the step-by-step process of designing a pop up ad and the same software will then give you an HTML code that you can paste onto your site or can have your web site designer paste the code onto the site. This pop up bonus will automatically appear when someone leaves your site. In other words, you do not have to have a high level of web design expertise to have a pop up on your site and it does not require any extra hosting expense or any extra advance level of hosting in order to have it on your site.

Chapter Sixteen

Since you know that your goal in business is to make money and in order to make money you need to be able to sell as many products or services as you can, then I am sure that you will agree with me regarding the next statement. Many people, even though after being explained, the facts do agree with me, but initially many people are reluctant to agree with the following statement.

Your entire web site should be devoted towards selling. Any element in your site that does not fulfill the act a turning a prospective visitor into a customer is useless and removed from the site. Now by saying this, I do not mean that you should not have a part of your site where people can leave testimonials. What I do mean is that if people leave testimonials, the page should be set up in such a way that when other customers visit, they should be encouraged to buy your products or services based on what they read. If you want to have a frequently asked questions section, make sure that it is specifically devoted towards selling the products or services that you offer. For instance instead of having questions set up that give people only general information have the Q & A section set up in a way that he information they are being given will encourage your customers to actually make a purchase. Everything on your site should be formulated with the ideas of leading your visitors into becoming customers.

The actual content on your web site should also be there not just to provide information but to providing information that will lead to sales. For instance, if you have a weight loss web site that sells weight loss supplements then you want to have articles on the different methods that could be utilized to lose weight make sure that the only methods that you cover are those which you have products or services based on those methods. Otherwise, you could easily write 100 different methods on weight loss but the only methods that you should be interested in tell your customers about your products or services. I am not telling you to lie and I am not telling you to omit any information. What I am telling you is to focus everything on your site into the selling process. If you do feel inclined to give your customers every means of losing weight make sure that every time you describe those methods that the products or services on your site should be supported by all of the content that is on your site. Your content on the site should always be geared towards people making a purchase.

If you have an article that tells people to walk everyday and that by walking everyday they will lose an average of 2 to 3 pounds a month, you need to explain that the most important element is for them to take action. Of course, the best action they can take is to purchase the supplements you have available on your site or to follow the guidance and instructions provided on your site.

Remember, even when you are giving information on your site, do not give away everything free. The more information that you give to your customers, the more encouraged they will be to stay on your site to read. Though if too much free information is given, they will not have any reason to actually pay for the products or services that you offer. What you want to do is always give people a taste of what you are offering without giving away the whole show. The same thing takes place when you go to see a movie. At the beginning, you will see the previews in which they show you enticing parts of an upcoming movie. What the movie studios do is to show you different scenes in previews that will appeal to different people based on the needs of the person if they are looking for a movie to make them happy or to have an escape or to have an intellectually stimulating experience. The producers are showing them small clips of the movie that will appeal to different people in the market place. They will not, however, show the most exciting parts of the movie, the conclusion or the climax because they know that if they give away too much, no one will have any need to actually pay for a ticket to see the movie.

You need to do the same thing on a web site. Make sure that you are offering enough information to make your visitors excited. Offer enough information to hook those visitors. Encourage your visitors to actually purchase your products or services. Any of the big movie studios such as Miramax, Disney, MGM or any other movie company will show you enough of the film to make you excited, showing you that it is an incredible film and worth spending your time and money to watch. However, they will not give away the truly integral parts of the movie so that you will come to the theater and pay for it.

You need to be able to demonstrate to your prospective customers how much they have to gain by utilizing your products or services. Make them excited by what you have to offer with informative articles, informative ad content and having advertisements geared to the needs and benefits of your customers. If applicable to you, you should provide pictures of products or services whenever possible. At the same time, these pictures will help sell the merchandise if they are not over done. Too many pictures will take away from the imagination and customers will not be able to envision themselves using the products. If you look at a clothing catalog, you will notice that they have models wearing the clothing but in only one or two pictures and not from every angle and in different situations. They want the clothing to look good and then leave the rest to the shopper's imagination since the shopper may be the person who will be wearing the clothing that is being showcased. When you do use pictures, make sure that they will enable you to sell. If they do not contribute to the selling process, then do not use them.

I have gone to many websites and I see a picture of either the site owner or the employees who work for the web site. Many times, this is the worst mistake that web site operators can make because if a customer comes to your site and they are expecting the site to be run by someone other than who is actually being pictured in the site, you may lose a sale. Let me give you an example. You could have a great web site teaching people how to go sailing. You may know everything about sailing but if you do not look like what people think the average sailor should look like, you do not want your picture to be posted on the web site. If you want your picture on the site because you feel that if people actually see who is behind the site they will be more willing to do business with you, that is a fair assumption, as long as a picture does match up with what the customers expect. If you are selling sailing products or a course on how to sail, make sure that in your picture you are dressed like a sailor so people can imagine you teaching them how to sail and can also perceive you as a reliable source of sailing products. Every time you use a picture of yourself on your site, ask yourself if this picture will actually in fact lead customers to decide to buy from you. If you are unsure then I advise against using the picture but what I would do is use a picture that does convey the feelings you want to come across to visitors. A picture works the same way as words do. Words, when formulated correctly and used properly help convince customers to buy from you because words elicit a certain image in the mind of a customer.

Pictures can do the same thing. The wrong use of a picture will lead to the loss of a sale while the use of the right picture will help to gain customers. Make sure that the people pictured in your pictures look real. Here is another problem that site operators run into. Many times, they try to use pictures of people who look too perfect for their role. People can notice the accuracy of pictures and most people will know if those people are models or if they are actually users of your products or services. The same is true of a testimonial. If the testimonial is not written by a real person who has actually experienced your products or services people will be able to see through that testimonial. On the other hand, if the testimonial is written by an actual user or if the picture is that of an actual user, then people will be able to pick up on the fact that these are legitimate. Your credibility will be higher in their eyes and you will be taken more seriously.

Keep in mind that with all of the fraud that unfortunately takes place in the marketplace, how important it is for you to be able to convey the feeling of legitimacy towards the users who visit your web site.

By keeping this in mind remember; in every component of your web site always make sure that it is aimed at selling. You do not need any fancy logos and you do not need any gimmicks. What you do need to do is have a web site that is based on selling. Any time your web site is based upon turning prospective customers into actual buyers, you are on the right track. I have visited many attractive web sites that have great 3D graphics and live videos featuring audio, but unless everything is geared towards selling, you will not make money with your web site. The actual key to selling online is stick with the basics and a very basic looking site that is aimed specifically towards selling the products or services you are offering.

Some of the best websites that I have seen on the market consists of a single sales page. When you arrive at the site all that you see is a single page with ad content explaining why people would benefit from the purchase of the products or services being offered. The site may have one or two pictures of the product or of people using the product but the site will not have any additional pages or pictures including graphics or animation. Some of those simple sale page websites are responsible for literally $10, 000.00 to $20,000.00 of sales per month. Some of those sites have an extremely high profit margin. The process by which they are selling the products or services is extremely effective. We will discuss later on what some of those sites are and how to emulate them. I will tell you that so far what you have learned is already enough information to put you close to the performance of those sites.

Chapter Seventeen

As we have illustrated throughout the discussion in this book, the communication between you and your customer is extremely important as it takes place online. It is generally the only communication that you are having initially with your customers. There will be a point in your communication when you are able to speak with your customers one-on-one or you may start exchanging e-mails, actually speaking on the telephone, or you may even meet with the customer in person. Up to that point, the only communication that the customer will have with you is the interaction on the web site. When a potential customer arrives at your web site, he or she will make a decision based on the information that they see before them on your site. If you want to have a good chance of turning a prospect into a customer, you need to use every opportunity as we have been discussing to sell the customer the benefits of your products or services.

From experience and the experience of other online entrepreneurs, I have found that their experience confirms my own experience, the more text that one has on a web site, the higher of a conversion ratio that there will be. This means that the more text it will translate into having a higher percentage of visitors turning into customers. The reason that this takes place is that your web site is acting as your salesperson. The more text contained on your site, the more of a sales pitch is being extended to the customers. Remember, you do not want the sales pitch to be clearly a sales pitch. You want it to be a subdued pitch that consists of practical information that the customer will be interested in reading. This way the prospects will continue reading all of the test that is on the site. At the same time remember, the more text that you have the more sales that you will obtain from those prospective customers. Even if a customer does buy a product or order a service from you, the more text that you have on the site will mean there will be a better chance of that customer ordering additional products or additional services.

The reason that having a lot of text on the site works is that because the more the customer reads, the more they can be convinced of the benefits of buying your products or services. The more you can show the customer in terms of words the more of a chance is that they will place an order with you.

If you examine some of the successful online campaigns, you notice that they consist primarily of text. The text surpasses the usage of pictures, graphics or any other fancy web site design. Many successful online sites heavily rely on their text and some of them, besides having one or two graphics on the site, do not have any other graphics or pictures but rely heavily on their text as their sales effort. This is because going back to the lessons that direct mail have taught us, and the lessons that were learned in the 1920's when advertisements were used heavily in newspapers and all types of media, the proven results determined that the more text that is written in an ad, the more serious it will be taken. Text was also proven as a defining reason that someone will be drawn to that advertisement.

Think about it this way. Imagine how hard it is to look at a page and not read the contents of the page. As a matter of fact, anytime you look at a letter, you will actually instantly read that letter. You will not just study the shape of the letter, but will actually read the letter and if there is a word before you then you read it. Think how hard it is just to study the shapes of words without actually reading them. After all, letters are just shapes and they are shapes to which we attribute sounds when in reality the letter A is no different from a similarly shaped pyramid. Of course, when we look at an A, we attribute the letter with the qualities of the letter as opposed to the qualities of a pyramid. We do not read the pyramid because it is not readable. What if we had learned that a pyramid was a letter? Then we would look at a pyramid and read it as a letter.

The same thing takes place when text is used in an advertisement. As soon as people see text, they read it. They have no choice due to conditioning. Therefore, one could look at a picture, glance at it once or twice, and not pay any attention to it or they may not even be drawn to the picture. Therefore, the entire purpose of having the picture on site will be lost. However, when you have text on your site the person glances at the text with no choice but to read what he sees, which is the text. As they read, the subconscious mind will absorb the sales message that you are introducing. At that point, if the person is interested in what you have to say then that person will act on your sales message and purchase the products or services.

When you see an advertisement in the newspaper, the advertisements that you are usually drawn to are not the ones with the pictures or graphics but the ones with plenty of text because you become curious as to why there is so much text and you want to know what is the story? People are drawn to stories. People want to be entertained and they want to be informed. Any time they see an ad with a lot of text, they will be very curious to discover what is it that is going on and requires so much text in the message. If a flyer only has two or three words on it you will assume that it is not important. On the other hand, if you see that the flyer is full of text you will be interested to see what the flyer is announcing.

The same principal takes place when a visitor comes to your web site. When they first arrive at your site, they will immediately decide if they want to continue to browse or if they want to move on and continue surfing. Studies have shown that an average visitor will make this decision within 15 seconds. You have 15 seconds to make a solid impression on a visitor. You do this by having a lot of text. As soon as they see the text, they will read the message out of curiosity. Of course, it has to be interesting or appealing to the visitor or of course, they will leave. If they arrive at your site and see very little text I can assure that they will assume the site has very little to offer and they will move to another site. You need to have plenty of interesting text to draw them in so that will continue reading.

Now that you can see the importance of having plenty of text on your site, you should also realize the importance of having a professional copywriter write the text for you. By this, I mean that there are people who are experienced in writing sales copy. They may write the sales copy for direct mail, advertisements in newspapers, mail order publications or for web sites since they have the expertise that is involved in creating sales copy. Writing sales copy does not just mean writing a lengthy sales letter and at the same time, it does not mean just writing motivational phrases. What it is means is the delicate balance between having a lot of text that draws in a reader and causes them to continue reading the message and at the same time it motivates them to take the action without over delivery on the point. If you over emphasize any point too much then the visitor will lose all interest. The person who is reading your sales copy has to be excited about what they are reading, interested in what they are reading and motivated to continue reading.

Make sure that you have an expert writing your sales copy who has experience in the field. That experience may be expensive and it will definitely cost money but I can assure that having a professional write the sales copy for you will pay off in the short-term and the long-term. Each time you receive a visitor to your site they will respond that much more favorably to your site depending on the level of expertise of the person who wrote the sales copy.

Therefore, in all of the sites I have had I either consulted with someone who wrote the sales copy or someone wrote the sales copy for me or I consulted with experts until I was able to develop my own level of necessary expertise to write my own copy. At that point, I started writing sales copy for other web site owners and for other people conducting online marketing campaigns because I had developed through trial and error and much hard word a level of expertise that was able to help people sell their products or services with my sales to copy. I will be the first one to admit that any time I write sales copy I consult with people who are more knowledgeable and more experienced because those people can help me write a successful ad copy. No matter how much you may know about writing sales copy there is always someone else who knows more than you do and in any case, it helps to have someone review my work. An independent party can usually notice what is lacking and make positive suggestions.

Chapter Eighteen

If you do decide that you want to use graphics on your site, make sure that the graphics are professional in appearance and that they contribute to the sales process. I do realize that there are times when graphics are not only helpful also essential to the products or services that you are offering. In that situation you will definitely want to use relevant graphics and I recommend that they are designed by someone who is not only a web site designer but also specifically a graphics designer. By this mean that if the person has web site design skills then it is a plus since they will be able to cohesively implement a graphic into your site. However, if the person does not have graphic design skills, then I would not use that individual. I would prefer to use the services of someone who is an expert graphics designer without any web site skills as opposed to using the services of someone who is a web site designer but is not primarily a graphics designer.

There are instances when you will need to use graphics. When you sell information online, you want to use a graphic that will be the cover of your book or illustrate what you are offering. If you sell something that is an intangible item such as software, information that is downloadable, or a program, artwork you need to be able to illustrate what you are selling without having a picture of the item. If you are selling downloadable information, you cannot show a picture of that information. If you display the information then you are actually giving away what you want to sell. If you are selling software, there is no actual picture of the software. If you are selling a computer program, the same applies. If you are selling artwork online, you do not want a picture of the actual artwork because then you are giving away free what you are trying to sell. All of these situations should make you have a graphic, which would represent to the people what you are selling.

Let's suppose that you are selling information that will be downloadable from your site directly to the user's computer. In this situation, what you are doing is selling the information as an e-book. You will want to have a graphic which will be the cover of your e-book or which will be a picture so to speak of the package of information that they are receiving. Picture it this way, if you saw a picture of a book on Barnes & Noble you would actually be looking at a color scan of the cover of the book. What you would want is to have a graphic designer create a cover for you that you can put on the web site so that people can look at the cover of the e-book and be motivated to buy your book due to the professional appearance of the cover of the e-book. You see, publishers realize this because when they publish a book, they don't just concentrate on the content of the book but they also concentrate on the design of the front and back covers, the illustrations, the layout, the typesetting and the spine. They realize that the cover is an extremely important element in the sales process of the book.

When you sell you book you want to have a great design on your site which will be the cover of your e-book to motivate sales. The same is true of selling software or computer programming. You need to have a graphic created that actually looks as if someone took a picture of the software box. Basically, you are creating something that does not exist and posting it on the web site so that people can get an idea of what they are buying. When you sell an intangible then you need to make tangible. You could be selling the best software on the market but if people cannot visualize what they are buying then they will be very reluctant to buy it.

If you think about a religious experience being very similar to this concept, you know that when praying you use visual and tangible effects in your mind to help you with the religious process. This does not mean that you pray to an object or use an object in order to pray. The mood that is created by certain objects or the atmosphere that is present helps you to pray because prayer is an intangible and having a tangible atmosphere is helpful to prayer.

The same is true of the sales process that takes place on a web site. Many of the products that are sold online and especially the services are sold online are intangibles. You will need to have graphics that will not only illustrate what you are selling but also will set the mood for what you are selling. Think about it this way, if you have a web site that is geared to a religious market then why not have graphics of perhaps the sun rising, a nature scene or of the sky. Any graphic will be fine if it gives people the idea that this is a religious web site or that would put people in the mood to be conducive towards making a purchase or responding to your religious web site. As you can see, graphics are extremely important because they are what people will respond to when there are no pictures to convey an intangible message.

Chapter Nineteen

Many products and services do allow for the taking of pictures and do allow the pictures to be a part of the sales process. If you are selling your handmade crafts online then you may want to take pictures of those crafts. If you are offering a service where you will do engraving for any jewelry that people send to you then you may want to have pictures of your shop where you do the work so that people can get the idea that you are a professional operation and you have all the tools available to do the work. Even though the service you are selling is an intangible, it is not a service that can be delivered, the end result is something that they can enjoy and benefit from but the actual service is intangible. When you are doing engraving, you want to be able to convey the image that the service they are purchasing is extremely valuable. You can take a picture of yourself actually working on engraving or of your employees who are also working.

If you offer tutoring online, you can have a picture of yourself tutoring a student. This way a student can get the idea that you are a teacher and they can visualize themselves being taught by you even if the teaching is only taking place online. If you are selling a car online or a computer online or a VCR then you will need pictures of the items so that people can get a better idea of what they are purchasing.

When you sell an item that is used you especially want to have plenty of pictures so that people will not be hesitant to buy a used item and they can see that the item you are offering is in good shape and they will receive an item that looks almost like new. If the item is blemished, you are fully disclosing that fact and the customer will not have to be concerned about any surprises that they might not see.

When you take pictures, you will need those pictures to meet a very high quality or otherwise you should not bother with pictures at all. Once there is a need for the pictures, it means that people will evaluate your products or services partially based on the pictures that they are looking at. Make sure that the pictures are of a very high quality. Make sure that the pictures that you are using are taken by a digital camera with a pixel of at least 3.0. The higher pixel is preferable but most digital cameras are quite expensive when you go over the 3.0 mark.

Taking pictures of your items is similar to any other service that you will be using to set up your online presence. As long as you can afford it and if it does not detract from paying for other service, I recommend that you go ahead and have a professional take pictures for you. Even if it is not a professional, have someone who has experience taking pictures or someone who enjoys taking pictures as a hobby. This person could have the same level of expertise as a professional would have. I strongly recommend that you have high quality pictures taken of your items or at least have a professional review your photographs because once you put those pictures online your potential customers will judge whether they should make a purchase from you based on the quality of your pictures. Remember, it is important to have good quality pictures because you want to avoid a situation where someone receives an order from you and then they complain afterwards because they feel that the pictures did not properly represent the products. You do not want to go through the hassle of the return process and take back the merchandise when the return could have been avoided. In any type of a situation where you will have merchandise that needs to be photographed before being sold online, make sure you use a good digital camera with a pixel range of 3.0 and make sure that they are good quality pictures.

Something that online entrepreneurs like to do is taking pictures with a regular camera and then scanning them into their web sites. This can be done as long as the scanner you are using is a very high quality one so it can pick up all of the details of the picture. At the same time, the camera that you used to take pictures of the items should also be a very high quality camera so that when they are scanned in they will look good.

If you ask me which I recommend more than the other is a digital camera or a high quality camera, I recommend the digital. You will avoid the expense of needing a scanner and you could look at the pictures as they are going to appear on the computer and you can decide immediately if you will keep that picture or delete it and retake the picture. With a digital camera, you can photograph it as many times as you want until you are 100% satisfied with the results. When you use a regular camera you will not know if the pictures are good until you have them developed which will waste a lot of time. Remember, if you are going to use pictures, ask yourself if those pictures will help you sell and if they are necessary for the sales process they will be a distraction and will take attention away from the quality. If the picture could lead to a direct sale then I strongly recommend that you use your pictures. The litmus test is always "does this item enable me to sell or will it detract from the sales process?"

Chapter Twenty

Any time that you are in a situation where you have to sell products or services, you are much better off using an emotional approach as opposed to the logical. In other words, you are better off appealing to your potential customers emotions than to their logic. The reason for this is that while a purchase might be logical or illogical, people do not rely on logic to make most of their purchasing decisions. In fact, there are studies that have been done to prove that people actually make their decisions based on emotion and then after use logic to rationalize their choice. In order for you to be a successful online entrepreneur, you need to be able to grasp the idea that in order to be successful while selling online that you need to appeal to people's emotions.

This does not mean that your offer should not be logical. Remember, people are logical and they will study and examine what you are offering using their logical abilities. On the other hand, they will be heavily influenced by emotions. In a situation where there are two online web sites selling the same product or service, the online web site that reaches out to people's emotions will have a much better chance of making the sale.

Think about how a sports team is marketed. One thing stressed is the loyalty connection between fans and their sports team. Sports teams spend millions of dollars developing this feeling of loyalty between their fans and the team. From a logical perspective, there is no reason why a fan needs to be anymore loyal to his local football team as opposed to a football team in another state. The fan may feel after thinking about it logically that he would rather support a team based at home as opposed to another state. This idea is fine as long as you remember that there really is not a logical reason why a fan needs to support a local team or any football team whatsoever. The support of that team will not lead to the actual success of the team and on the other hand, the life of that sports fan will not be any worse off if the fan does not support the team. The nature of people is that they want to be emotionally involved with a person, an object, or an idea.

Therefore, the top marketers in the business environment always make sure to appeal to people's emotions while they are selling.

What are some of the emotions to which you should be appealing? Appeal to the emotion of love, the desire to be perceived as an equal, the view of gratitude, the concept of happiness, the longing for safety, or the sense of being a part of a group or serving a greater purpose. All of these emotions are common to everyone and each of these emotions is developed differently. Some of us may have a larger desire to find someone to love. Others may have a larger desire for safety. This depends on upon which society we are marketing, where the people live geographically and also the culture of the people. Everyone has a desire to satisfy his or her need for companionship. Someone living in an upscale New Jersey area may not feel the need for safety as much as someone living in a rural area where there are bears roaming or foxes at night and they even spot a wolf once in awhile. That person will have a much bigger need for safety and that person will respond to sales efforts for products that ensure safety. This could be alarms, outdoor lights or emergency generators. While the person living in an upscale area could live in a million dollar mansion with every alarm system available but if they are alone then their need for companionship will be very great. You can market to that individual living in New Jersey social events that take place or dating books, clothing, perfume or cologne that will help that individual meet someone else. Both people, including the person in the rural area and the person who lives in upscale New Jersey, sometimes both of those markets can be equal. On the other hand, some people, no matter where they live, will always feel safe and always have companionship. You need to study your market very carefully. You must determine what your market is truly seeking, what products or services they really need and what emotions they need to have satisfied.

If you are marketing to the singles group then you should be selling products and services that focus on the benefits that your products can offer an individual which they need to find a person with whom they can begin a relationship. If you are marketing to investors who are nearing retirement, then you want to market products or services that will appeal to their emotional desire for stability, safety and well-being. You could market to them conservative mutual funds, high yielding CD bank accounts or bonds. Regardless of what you are marketing from your web site, a banner ad, or an e-zine, make sure to focus on the emotional component that the product or service can fulfill. Also, make sure that you focus on what emotional benefit your customer has in mind when they consider purchasing your products or services.

Let's say you are marketing cologne. Think about the emotional benefit for the purchaser of the cologne is looking to buy. Someone who buys cologne most likely has two reasons, one is that they like to smell good, which cannot be the real reason because they could take a shower, use a good shampoo and they will smell fine and be clean. Another component is because they are aware that the better they smell the better chance there is for them to attract the opposite sex and if they meet someone to date or someone they are already involved with they feel that by smelling better they will be able to appeal to the other person.

When you market your products or services make sure to keep in mind the true reasons why someone would want to purchase your products or services. If you have a web site devoted to perfumes, you do not just stress the types of perfumes that you offer and you do not stress only the smell of the perfumes. Rather you would stress the emotional benefit that they can deliver. One of those emotional benefits here is that this perfume will help people attract the opposite sex and will help them to have better relationships they are involved with.

Another example would be a web site devoted to selling flashlights. Flashlights have a very practical purpose and enable someone to see in the dark. Now the emotional benefit that someone is looking to gain with a flashlight is the feeling of safety because if they are in the dark in an emergency they can use this flashlight to see in the dark. If they are stuck in the dark on a road and they are waiting on help or need to repair their car, they can use that flashlight. The flashlight is then giving them a strong sense of safety, which is one of the primary reasons, why people buy flashlights. You would therefore want to stress the emotional benefits fulfilled by someone buying the flashlights you have to offer.

People also have emotional needs from the products or services that you offer. Let's say that you have a book which teaches English to immigrants. There are two ways to go about marketing this online. You can stress all of the benefits that this book has such as enabling people to learn English in a short period of time. You can stress all of the grammar and the vocabulary that a reader will learn. You could stress how easy it is for someone to use your book. These are all great things to stress and are important for those customers to know from a logical perspective but remember, you first need to capture their emotions and after that, you can focus on the logical reasons. Why would an immigrant want to buy a book that will teach them how to learn English?

Well what are the emotional needs that an immigrant has? They want social acceptance, they need to be involved with people around them, they need to develop connections to their new country and they need money and food and the best way to get this is to learn the language and get a job or start a business and without being fluent in English this will be very difficult. Another emotional need is the need for love and if they want to form a relationship with some one in the United States, they will need a book to teach them how to speak English.

As you can see, there are many reasons why you should stress the emotional benefits and look for the needs that your products or services can meet. You will have a better chance to sell your products or services because of the strong appeal that it has if it is aimed at their emotions.

Chapter Twenty-One

Any successful marketing campaign needs to know what its conversion ratio is in order for it to be successful. If you want to run a successful online business, you must understand and determine your conversion ratio. By this I mean a conversion ratio is simply keeping track of the visitors that your site receives, not just the hits but also the unique visitors and then determine what percentage of your unique visitors actually make a purchase of your products. The conversion ratio is not just a term of sales. You want to use it in terms of obtaining prospects for your business. You will use it in terms of keeping track of your sales leads, how many people open your e-mails, and how many respond to your e-mails and how many request further information. You will also need to study it in terms of how many times does it take for you to contact a prospect until they give you their information and how many times does it take to contact the prospect until they become a customer.

The reason that all of this is important is because in order for you to be successful online, you need to spend money to market your web site. Therefore, you need to be able to study the conversion ratio very carefully. If you are selling a product that gives you a $50.00 profit per sale, then in order for you to successfully sell it online, you need to make sure your total advertising costs related to the one sale is under $50.00. Not only should the cost be under $50.00 but you also need to insure that the cost including your other expenses of running your business is still well under $50.00.

First, let's assume the average cost of running your business every month is $100.00, which includes a hosting fee, a telephone line for the business, your local and long distance bill, faxes, cost of having to make copies, and many other miscellaneous costs. When you run an online business, most of your costs will be covered by the customer. Either you will be charging the customer for shipping or the price of your products or services will include shipping or servicing charges. In other words, your only cost will be your actual costs of running a business and in most situations you can run it from your house or as a side venture from your current job then you really will not have any sizeable costs associated with it. However, the cost that will be present in your business and may actually grow as your business grows is advertising costs.

Previously we discussed methods for eliminating or reducing your advertising costs as your business grows. Initially, when you start out, you will have to spend advertising dollars. Let's assume that you notice for every 100 visitors you receive to your site, that one visitor makes a purchase. This meaning to you is that it takes 100 visitors to get one sale and receive a $50.00 profit. You know that you can spend up to $45.00 or up to even $49.00 and still be profitable. You must decide on what kind of profit margin that you want to run your business. If you want a 100% profit margin that means that if your costs are $25.00 you want your profit to be $25.00. This is possible but what we need to do is know that the most we can spend on a visitor is .25 cents because it will take 100 visitors to produce the sale, which gives us a profit, and we want 100% profit over the cost of the advertising. If we spend 25 cents in attracting each visitor your profit will be $25.00 per 100 visitors. Now that is a great number to work with. If you are attracting 1,000 visitors a week, those visitors are costing $250.00 in terms of advertising. Those 1,000 visitors in terms of a conversion ratio of 1% are producing 10 sales, which equals $500.00. Now $500.00 a week may not sound like a lot but when you multiply the $500 a week times 52 weeks a year you get $26,000.00. As you can see, it can become a sizeable amount of money especially if your business is part time or if it is money earned in addition to your present source of income.

You do not need to stop there since once you develop a system that works and you know how to increase your advertising to attract more visitors to your site, you could run the business exponentially. You could start advertising to the extent that you would be able to every week bring in not 1,000 visitors but 10,000 visitors. If you can get 10,000 to your site per week and still maintain your 1% conversion ratio and your cost is .25 cents per visitor, you are now talking about $2,500.00 of advertising per week. This is producing a profit of 100 sales times $50.00, which is $5,000.00, subtract the $2,500.00 in advertising and this leaves $2,500.00 per week. That is a sizeable amount of money as you are surely aware.

As you can see, the best part of running an online business is that you never have to leave your full time occupation. You can set your well running system on "auto pilot" meaning every month you renew your advertising. Every week you continue your advertising strategy and then as the money flows in you reapply a portion of that money to advertising for the next month. This system will mean you only need to spend a couple of hours per week to insure that things are running smoothly. You may want to hire an assistant at some point or someone to work part time with you to process orders.

Let's study the conversion ratio further now. Let's say that you have a marketing campaign and it is a two-step process. The first part is focused on generating leads and then there is a following campaign to produce sales for those weeks. For example, you have an e-zine, which is an e-mail newsletter and you send it out to an e-mail list of 20,000 names. You can buy e-zine lists, you can build your own lists or you can form a joint venture and use someone else's list to send out your e-mails. Let's say they have a list of 20,000 people and suppose you pay them $100.00 to send out your e-mail. Out of those 20, 000 people you need to study how many people respond and how many of those will actually become customers and this is how you determine if it is worthwhile to advertise using that person's list. How do we do this? First, we study and we do not try it with a list of 20, 000 people but we try with a much smaller list so it will be less costly. I suggest trying it out for the first time that you purchase a list or an advertisement that reaches 2,000 prospects. This is a good enough number to gauge a response. This is a targeted list that was assembled from people who are specifically interested in your products or services and you will know that they will be interested at least in the topic with which you are dealing.

Let's say your site is devoted to selling printed Tee shirts and they have logos from WWII and you are appealing to people who are interested in that era such as veterans, collectors or just anyone in general who is interested in the era. Now you verify your list of responses against the 2,000 people and find that 100 people responded by sending you an e-mail inquiring and asking for more information. The next step is that you will send them another letter and direct them to your web site to close the sale. Usually this two-step approach is used when the products or services are more expensive.

Instead of the product being a printed Tee shirt, let's make it a personal computer which is loaded with software and it is aimed at educators and the software will be set up to enable them to teach classes better and prepare exams or review class material. Now this e-mail list of 2,000 educators is perfect for you because it is aimed specifically at the market with which you are dealing. You would then set up your e-mail to explain the benefits that educators can receive from the computer and make sure it appeals to the emotional benefits that they need to receive. At the same time, you would show how this computer would satisfy all of their needs. We know that an educator needs to do a better job of teaching people, preparing for class. The benefits that they are looking for are to be able to know and have the satisfaction of having taught the students well. They could obtain a raise by becoming a good educator. They could receive recommendations from their students or other teachers and praise from the parents of the students. With all of this in mind, you want to create a good advertisement e-mail that will reach them and appeal to all of their needs.

You send out this e-mail to 2,000 educators whom we know should have a basic interest in your offering. Out of those 100 respond to the e-mail and ask for more information. We know to begin with that we have a 5% response based on people who are looking for more information. Next, you would contact those educators either on the phone or by e-mail back and forth or faxing more information. The value of a two-step campaign is that you do not lose a sales lead simply if they are not initially interested in what you are offering.

At this point, you notice that within a month from the 100 people who contacted you then you have 10 sales. This makes the conversion ratio on your sales effort is 10%. Looking back, what you are able to obtain initially is a 5% conversion ratio as far as taking people who are interested in your offering into a lead and then another 10% conversion ratio and actual sale of that products or services. The reason why at this point your conversion ratio and actual sales is so high because they are people who already expressed an interest in what you are offering. They put in the effort of contacting you to get more information and now it is just a matter of actually convincing them to purchase the computer. This is usually not that hard as long as you are offering something that they really need and as long as what you are offering actually matches up with what they understand when they contacted you. Your actual profit from this campaign will be $1, 500.00 and of course will take a lot more time.

Since your return is $1, 500.00 you can spend anything up to an amount that will still give you a profit that is suitable for you. So if you would be happy with a total profit of $1, 000.00 after having spent all of your time communicating and sending e-mails or price sheets or allowing them to use the software online, then you know that you can spend up to $500.00 doing your marketing. Another way is that once you have determined what your profit for this type of undertaking must be, you can also be proactive and spend money on much large marketing campaigns. You know what your average profit will be and now you can afford to market not just to 2, 000 people but you can afford to market to 20, 000 people or 200, 000 people as long as you have the resources to answer all of the inquires that you will receive and that you have the ability to actually close the sale. Remember, you can pay for a large advertising campaign and in your mind you can figure out the numbers and that you will have a high enough conversion ratio so it will be worth spending the money and as you solicit the leads you will be able to close sales on the leads. As you remember, everything that you do in business actually requires work and effort so if you do not have the ability or the people to help close the sales then it is not worth it to spend the money on a large advertising market campaign. Regardless if you are now selling a product which is downloadable directly from your web site, which would not require any mailing or any processing of the order or if you are sending out an order that actually needs to be processed there will be plenty of other associative work. You will need people sending e-mail for immediate interest, there will be telephone calls as well and if you don't stay on top of the e-mail and phone calls not only will those people not buy from you but you might develop a reputation as being unreliable or unprofessional. The most important part is actually being able to develop a strong reputation because even if those customers do not order from you today, later on they may hear from someone else that you have a good reputation they will be more likely to buy from you.

Going back to the conversion ratio, you need to be able to keep track of this ratio as it pertains to every aspect of your marketing campaign. This will pertain to the actual selling of your products, soliciting leads and closing the sale since you have a marketing campaign that is able to produce a very large number of responses. If you do not have the ability or the time to close on the responses then the marketing campaign is worthless. Meaning, you could have a banner ad or an ad that produces a high number of responses but if you do not close on any of those responses then your advertising money was wasted. Therefore, when you have a marketing campaign you need to make sure that the campaign is targeted and specifically aimed at the market you are interested in and at the people who are exposed to your advertisement understand exactly what you are offering.

Here is an example. If you have a marketing campaign that is geared towards a health product and the product specifically helps people who cannot sleep at night. The nutrient in your product is going to enable them to relax and fall asleep easier than they could in the past. This is what you need to let your customers know. If you only advertise, "I can help you sleep better at night." Then you have a banner ad so that people can arrive at your site by clicking on it and see that your site is not what they expected, they will simply leave the site and your experience with that visitor is not going to be valuable to you. On the other hand, if you advertise an offer online that you have a web site that says "E-mail me to discover the best way to fall asleep tonight without any problems." People will not understand what you are offering. You will receive many e-mails from people who are looking for a better mattress, better heating in their house, a better pillow, or a vitamin that will help them relax but not have anything to do with helping them sleep. You might get replies from people who are having financial problems and understand your ad as being a product or service that is going to help them financially. If, on the other hand, you are extremely specific about what you are offering, you will receive a much smaller number of leads but those leads will be much more targeted. If your web site says, "Contact me for the best nutritional solution for a good night of sleep tonight." Then you need to give those people more information about what it is you are offering and how it will help them because you also want to make sure that the people who are in the market for the product or service that you are offering are willing to use your product or service that you are offering. Many people might want to get better sleep at night but are unwilling to take vitamins or nutritional supplements. If you are able to determine this, then not only will you have a higher conversion ratio but also the leads that you receive will be that much more valuable and the leads will be likely serious leads. Therefore, you may spend more money obtaining those leads as long as you know that the leads that you do receive are directly targeted. You also want to make sure that you are still spending the right amount of money so that you remain profitable while obtaining the leads and you must make sure that you are receiving enough leads to make your business viable. I would go so far as to say that even if your online business is not bringing enough leads to give you a full time income, but it is still bringing you enough targeted leads to make the business profitable then it is worthwhile to pursue that business in that fashion as opposed to developing a business where you are bringing in a lot of leads and spending a lot on advertising but your actual rate of return is very small. The reason I say this is that a web site that is bringing in a small number of leads that requires a small number of advertising expenses is going to give you a good profit. With the money that you are able to free up and do not have to spend on advertising, you will have a more consistent profit and devote that money to finding another source of advertising or develop a second online business which would help further your income.

As you can see already from this chapter, it is very important to be able to study your sales to conversion ratio and all of your conversion ratios so that you determine how much money to spend on advertising efforts and so that you can actually determine what your profit is compared to advertising.

To summarize, if you have a product or service that gives you a $20.00 profit then you want to have a 100% mark up, the most should spend on advertising is $10.00. If you have a product or service that appeals to a wide audience and it does not require a lot of effort to close the sale or deliver the product or service, then you would not mind closing the gap between your cost and your profit because you want to work on volume. If you are selling your product and it will give you a $10.00 profit (let's say that it retails for $20.00 and you know that there is an overwhelming demand in the market place) then you should be willing to sell the product at the same price because you are obtaining a $10.00 profit and you should be willing to spend up to

$15.00 advertising the product or even up to $18.00. As long as it remains profitable, you can reach hundreds of thousands of consumers and your business will become sizeable.

In other words, if you are selling a special pot that help people cook and it will allow them to cook a meal in half the time as before and it will give the food a great taste and you know that there are literally 200, 000 people out there who are specifically interested in the cooking pot. Then I think that it is safe to say that you would rather spend more money on your advertising so that you get 10% of those people to become your customers than to spend less money on your advertising and have a higher profit margin but only have a few hundred customers as opposed to 10% of 100, 000 which would mean 10, 000 customers. Alternatively, 10% of 200, 000 customers would give you 20, 000 customers. I am sure that you would rather earn $2.00 from every customer if you have 10, 000 than to have 100 customers and make a $10.00 profit from each one.

Basically, everything is in the numbers and you need to be able to study and understand your numbers clearly. Many of the online companies who fail do so specifically because they did not keep track of the conversion ratios. What ended up happening is that they spent a lot more money on their advertising than they should have. Not only did they do this, but also as they were generating revenue, they did realize what the revenue was actually costing them. If they had understood what the revenue was costing, they could pursued alternative marketing strategies that would enabled them to have the same number of customers and the same amount of revenue but it would have cost them less. Therefore, understanding your sales conversion ratio and understanding your general conversion ratio is extremely important. This way you could always determine if your online campaign is profitable, where you money is better spent. You might have a better conversion ratio when it comes to paper clip search engines as opposed to banner ads. On the other hand, you may have a better conversion ratio when you send out e-mail newsletters as opposed to paying for e-mail in someone else's newsletter. At the same time, you could also determine if you are headed in the general right direction. If you see that you are not obtaining the profit that you are looking for then you need to market a different product, service online, or you need to go to an entirely different online business venture. Therefore, if you understand this concept you will already be years ahead of other online entrepreneurs who have very good businesses plans but were unable to correctly implement the plan in respect to advertising.

Chapter Twenty-Two

One of the most effective methods to advertise online is using paperclip search engines. A paperclip search engine is basically a search engine that allows advertisers to bid on the right for appearing in a certain order under listings.

When visiting search engines like Yahoo! or AOL you will notice that for the most part as long as a web site meets certain criteria then the web site will appear under the search listing for certain terms. The ranking of those websites depends on many factors such as links that point to the site concerning the level of content related to the topic that is being searched. At the same time, there are websites like Overture.com or Google where websites can bid for the right to appear in the search listings. This means that if you do an online search for fax machines an AOL then the websites will show up are usually the sites that have the highest content relation to the term "fax machine" and they will be websites that have the most links pointing to them who deal in fax machines. If you go to Overture.com or Google, in Google the general sites still work the same way as does AOL and Yahoo! concerning the content and by the number of links pointing to the site but Google has a section called "Ad Words" which is a column that appears to the right of the search listing and you need to pay to appear over there. If you have a web site that caters to persons who want to purchase fax machines you can bid in the Google Ad Word program and have your site appear as #1 in the right column next to the regular listings anytime anyone searches for the term "fax machines".

What Overture.com does is actually pretty interesting because they have all of their listings being sponsored by advertisers. This means as soon as you search for "fax machines", every listing that appears on Overture.com is listed according to the level of bidding that was done for the position in the listing. Therefore, if you have a site that sells fax machines you can bid 30 or 40 cents to be the #1 spot on Overture.com. I am not sure what the actual cost is for bidding for the #1 is because the cost changes on a daily basis and there are many other related terms.

You do not specifically have to bid on the term "fax machines", you could for instance bid for the word "fax", or the term "fax service". The point is that by using Overture.com someone could go to search engine and could bid for the right to be the "Number 1" listed site for terms or phrases. The good thing about Overture.com is that they take the top three listings for every search and they put them on Yahoo!, AOL and many other search engines and each engine is compensated for allowing the search listing to appear on their sites. So if you go to Overture.com and you search for fax machines the first site that appears (let's call it "faxmachine.com"). Then when you go to Yahoo! The first site that also will appear is "faxmachine.com"; therefore, you get plenty of exposure by being listed on Overture.com, one of the top three spots.

Now the only problem to consider is that is extremely expensive to be listed for the top searches. Remember, as an advertiser you will pay not every time that your site appears in a listing but every time someone actually clicks on your listing. If you own the site "faxmachine.com" and you bid 40 cents for the right to appear in the #1 spot, you will actually pay 40 cents everyone clicks on your listing. Therefore, if the term fax machine gets 20,000 searches a month for the top three spots and you have 10, 000 people clicking on your site, then you will have an estimated bill of $4,000.00 per month. Now, that is fine as long as the profit that you are getting from your web site is over the $4, 000.00 per month. That is why we discussed in an earlier chapter that you should understand this in your conversion ratio. As long as you understand how much advertising money that you can afford to spend to generate a sale or how much advertising that you need to generate to produce a sale, then you should not feel intimidated by the high cost Overture.com charges when it comes to marketing or obtaining a listing on the search engine results.

Overture.com has a search tool that allows you to see two things…how much people are paying for each spot in a listing and also how many people are searching for a certain term or phrase. The reason that this is important is because when you are trying to decide how to market a product or service you can see when using Overture.com how many people actually search for that product, phrase, idea, term or concept and then you can determine if there is a big enough market for you to sell your product at a profit. Even if there is a small market and it is not expensive to advertise to that market, then it may be worthwhile. Even the word "expensive" is not that appropriate when discussed this way. What is more appropriate is knowing your conversation ratio and then the word "expensive" is only in relation to your conversion ratio, meaning that if it takes 100 customers to buy 1 fax machine then the fax machine gives you a profit of $40.00. This would mean that it is too expensive to bid 40 cents to get the #1 spot. On the other hand, if it only costs 10 cents to be on the #1 spot then it would be worth it because 100 visitors will cost $10.00 and your profit will be $30.00 per machine sold, providing that the entire $40.00 is profit from the sale of the fax machine.

What you can do when using Overture.com is that you do not need to only bid on actual terms or phrases that represent the products or services that you are selling. You can also bid on related terms or phrases that are aimed at the same market of interest for which your customers are looking. For example, it will cost a certain amount of money to bid for the term "fax machine" but I am sure that it is going to cost you less to bid for the term "buy a fax machine". Most people who search for fax machines will type in "fax machine" as opposed to the larger phrase so less people will be conducting a search. The mistake that most Overture.com users make and the people who use the Ad Word program in Google is that they spend all of their money on only one term which they feel will produce the highest number of results. What these people forget is that bidding on the term that has 10, 000 visitors is the same as bidding on 10 words at 1,000 visitors each. Even though it may seem to take longer to generate the same results because one word is exposed to 10, 000 people but one word isn't going to expose you to 1, 000 people ten times over, however, this is all happening on a monthly basis. Each of those terms is being searched 1,000 times every month and there-fore should cumulatively be reaching the same amount of people looking at your term. If you spend 10 cents on each term, each one is going to be searched 1,000 times, and your conversion ratio is still the same, you will come out ahead. Let us assume that your term is searched a total of 1,000 times and it is costing you 10 cents. You are actually spending $100.00. If your conversion ratio is 1% then you 10 people purchasing you product giving you a $4.00 profit, which equals $400.00. If you bid on, let's say, the #10 spot for the term "fax machine" mean-ing that you are actually saying to yourself "It's too expensive for me to have the #1 spot on a search term many times during the month so I will take the #5 spot, which is substantially cheaper." By having the #5 spot you may only receive 1, 000 hits on your site, meaning it is the same number of hits as if you took 10 dif-ferent terms that were searched a lot less. If the #5 spot costs you 20 cents then if is actually cheaper to take ten different terms and to bid only 10 cents to be in the #1 spot for those terms. Remember, I would rather be #1 on 100 terms that are being searched even if all of the terms are only being searched 40–50 times as opposed to being the #10 spot or the #20 spot under a term that is being searched thousands and thousands of times every day. Statistically speaking the top three results are visited by 80% of the visitors who are searching for a term. The next 4-5 spots have another 10% of the visitors and then the remainder of the spots has an insignificant number. Therefore, you would rather be in the #1 spot for terms that are not being searched that often only because you have a higher guarantee or higher likelihood of receiving more visitors. Even if there are only 100 people using the term "how to buy the best fax machines available online today" and the term only receives 50 visitors a month, but being in the #1 spot for that term you will have 80% of the visitors who are searching for that term. Eighty Percent of 50 people is 40 people and 40 times 100 terms is 4,000 visitors per month. A term like that is probably not even bid on so you could pay as little as 5 or 10 cents.

Besides Overture.com there are hundreds of other paperclip search engines which charge even less. The #1 terms, or the terms that are searched the most often online can be either gambling sites, investment site, business opportunity sites or any other kind of site the bidding and words associated with those sites are always going to be expensive regardless of which search engine you choose. If you look for terms or phrases that are related to the sites and look for terms that are not searched as often then you should go to other paperclip search engine besides Overture.com or Google you will be able to obtain the #1 spots in many instances for as low as

1-2 cents for every hit. Would not you rather have 10, 000 visitors coming to your site and each visitor only costing you a penny as opposed to having a higher volume of visitors in a shorter period of time with those visits costing you 40–50 cents each?

If you do have a product that you believe has very high conversion ratio or you do determine that it has a very high conversion ratio and you would rather work a slow profit for a much higher volume, then you might want to take the #1 spot even if the #1 spot is going to be expensive. I was selling a product online that gave me a profit of approximately $30.00. At the time, I was willing to spend up to $20.00 advertising that product and $20.00 meant that it cost me 20 cents per bid to get the #1 spot. I was willing to do that because I was able to generate a high volume of sales on a daily basis. I continued that campaign until the market reached became so saturated and I noted that customers had stopped buying the product. Therefore, I decided to move on to the next product for online sale. That is also something to remember with your own online campaign. Your marketing will always be limited. Your market may consist of hundreds of thousands of customers, billions of customers or only 100 customers, but there is a limit to the product that you are selling. You need to be able to monitor the products of your campaign very carefully because as you see your sales slowing down do not wait to spend money advertising your products or services until you have more customers. The last portion of your advertising whether in a paperclip search engine or a banner ad will be wasted instead. Once you notice that your sales are nearing 10% of their peak sales level then you should move on to another product or service offer online.

With the previous example when I was making $30.00 in profit per product, since I wanted to have the larger volume that I was able to produce and because it did make a difference and I was able to provide a high volume, I bid on the #1 spot and was willing to spend more money. However, if I would have produced the same result as I did with other products or services by being in the #1 spot for a highly visible search term as opposed to having the #1 spot for 100 different lesser visited search terms, than I would rather take the lesser visited search terms because it would cost me less and at the end of the day I would still receive the same number of visitors than if I was in the more expensive spot. The key is to always try to obtain the highest volume that you can and advertise in the most effective way and to keep track of actual number results. You must be honest with yourself in determining where you are actually making money and which campaign is more valuable.

Another reason why you should use a paperclip search engine is that they deliver specific traffic. The traffic is specifically interested in what you have to offer. When you bid on a term and people see the site listing, they see the name of your site and also a short description of your site. You can either write that description or have someone who works on writing sales copy to write the description for you. The description will be three to four lines under the products or services that your to which your web site caters. The reason that you need a very specific description that people will understand and will know what is being referenced because every click that you receive costs you money. A single click may not be that expensive but remember we are talking about not just reaching a point where you are receiving 100 visitors a day but you are receiving 1, 000 or 5, 000 a day. At that time, your advertising costs will be much higher.

You must be very clear to people what the products or services you are offering on your site. The actual traffic that arrives at your site will be that much more targeted. I remember coming across a web site that was extremely specific with the words that had been formed. They were terms that were directly associated with the insurance of the market that the site was catering to and at the same time, in reading the description of the site, it was offering a book to help people who were going through a divorce or considering a divorce. People who saw the site description understood exactly what information the book offered and the purpose of the book. It was not enough just to tell people that there was a book on divorce being offered but I believe that the point of the book was to help people avoid getting divorced and it was understood specifically what was being offered. Not only were the people who going through divorce interested, but the people who actually wanted to find a way out or those who wanted to avoid getting divorced were the most attracted to the book. This site had a sales conversation ration of 7%, meaning that for every 100 visitors to the site, seven people became customers. The product that they were selling gave them a $25.00 profit and they were spending 15 cents on advertising per visitor. That means that 100 visitors cost the site $15.00. Because they had a sales conversion ratio of 7% and the profit per item was $25.00, they were able to make $175.00 profit per every 100 visitors that came to the site. If you take $175.00 and subtract from it the $15.00 it cost for the 100 visitors then you are left with a profit of $160.00. Multiply this number time 1, 000 visitors or times 10, 000 visitors. Even if the site only received 1,000 visitors per month, it is still a great profit at $1, 600 per month. Multiply this by 12 months it would be over $17, 000 per year in profit just from a simple site that does not take any extra work or extra time.

Regardless of what you are selling when using a paperclip search engine make sure that your term is very specific to the market that you are looking for and that the description of your site is also very specific to the market that you are trying to reach. If you are not careful about this, then you will be able to take a lot of traffic but that traffic will not be targeted and therefore the visitors will not respond to the products or services that you are offering.

Many online marketers try to work on numbers, meaning that they just want as many people as possible to come to their site and are working on the premise that once people are on the site, regardless of what their actual primary interest is, they will have great ad content and sales copy on their site that they will be able to convince a certain percentage of those visitors to buy the products or services. Rarely does this strategy work because not only is it extremely difficult to create an interest when there is no interest but you also cannot take people who are not interested in what you are offering to get interested at the wrong time. These online marketers run into two challenges. One, they receive visitors who have no interest in the products or services that they are offering and even if those people are interested in what is being offered, if they are not interested in it at that time they will respond positively to the offer. What you need to do is be very specific in what you are offering on your site so that people will only come to your site when they are interested in what you are offering and when they are in the mood to get more information or to purchase.

If you follow these rules very closely not only will you have a successful online campaign but you will be able to get the most money out of your advertising whether it is from paperclip search engines or banner ads.

Chapter Twenty-Three

One of the most innovative and successful methods for marketing online is the use of joint ventures. This is the combination of two parties joining their efforts, resources and expertise to successfully market a product or service online. The reason for joint ventures being so successful is that both parties have a personal interest in seeing the product or service sell well online. A joint venture is not paying someone to advertise your products or services, is not setting up a deal where your products or services will be marketed, and is not advertising each other's products together in hopes of getting online business for both from a marketing campaign. A joint venture is actually when two parties bring into the equation an asset that the other party does not have and that only through the combination of those two assets, can there be a successful outcome.

In other words, let's say that you have a web site and it is devoted to selling DVD's online. These DVD's are geared toward the Spanish speaking market. You already have a great web site, you have a professional writer for ad copy, you have great Spanish movies but you do not know how to reach their market. You could advertise with some on paperclip search engines, you could write articles for other people's e-zines, you could pay to place ads in the e-zines, you could set up banner ads, however you still need to find a way to reach your consumers directly and you want to be able to reach a large number of your potential customers.

So what can you do? Well, to start you can find someone who has a web site that is catering towards the Spanish marketplace and more specifically to the marketplace within the marketplace that would be interested in Spanish movies that your are offering. You would contact an operator of the web site and ask if you could market your DVD's on their web site and give them a sure percentage of all of the sales that you make. The reason why the operator of that web site would be glad to do so is that now he has another product or service that can be sold through the web site. If they have a web site that is receiving 10, 000 hits a month and you can sell to 1/2% of those visitors then it is a great source of income for the operator of the web site and for yourself. Even if you are giving up a percentage of your profits, you will still end up having an increase of sales. Even thought the operator of the site is not being paid for his advertising expenses on the site, he is basically giving away that space on the site away free instead of charging. However, the operator of the web site is gaining because your product is now another source of revenue. Even if only 30 DVD's are sold a month, the web site operator will have a profit of $5.00 each which equals $150.00 per month. If he has a web site with 100, 000 visitors, and there are many sites which do, he could develop an extra source of income that could add up to $1, 000.00 per month. For you this is great because even though you are making less profit on each DVD, you also have an extra $1, 000.00 coming in from profits. The best joint ventures are where the profits are being split 50:50. This way both parties feel that they are receiving their fair share and either party will argue as far as to assets that they are bringing into the joint ventures relationship. You do not want either party to say, "Look, I am providing more, I am delivering more, therefore I should have a higher share of the profits." What I am concerned about is not which party is right, which party is entitled to higher percentages because these are small details. What I am concerned about is that through all of the discussions, which will turn into arguments; this joint venture will be dissolved and may never even have taken off in the first place. The best policy for joint ventures is from the very beginning to set up a 50:50 agreement where both parties know that they will be receiving half of the profits.

The next step is that you need to be sure that both parties have something invested into the joint ventures. It does not have to be financial but it has to be a firm commitment. By this I mean that the operator of the web site that is currently receiving the traffic from the Spanish market needs to commit to having an ad or having your DVD's featured on the site for a minimum period that you will agree on beforehand. At the same time, you have to make a commitment to sell the DVD's through that person's site for that period of time.

The reason why you need both parties to commit ahead of time, is not just because it will insure honesty or will insure that the joint venture runs smoothly, but any time that someone has something invested in a business arrangement then that person has more of an incentive to make sure that the business venture goes well. It is only human that if someone has something invested in an activity or a venture then he or she will try that much harder to make sure that the venture goes well.

Meaning, if you have a joint venture between a web site devoted to people who have clean teeth and a second party with special toothpaste that helps with teeth cleaning, you have a potential match. Let's say the operator of the web site has an e-mail list of 50, 000 people and the person who has the toothpaste product wants to sell it on the other site. An arrangement can be made in which their e-mail will be sent out to the 50,000 people on the list and product will be featured along with the benefits of using the toothpaste. Both parties need to do two things but before they do anything, they need to have an agreement in writing because it will save many headaches later on in the future. They now need to make a time agreement regarding how many times the e-mail will be sent. Will it be a one-time thing or will it be sent five times? Will there be five different articles, will there be three-four articles with the fourth actually featuring the product and allowing people to purchase the toothpaste?

There will have to be a solid commitment from the person who has the toothpaste to process a certain number of orders, to be available to respond to inquiries and to put his energies and resources aside to fulfill the orders. The operator of the web site is sending out the e-mail and it will tarnish his reputation if he sends out the e-mail and the product is then not available when people order it. Both ends of this deal need to make sure that they are committed to the process and they both have something invested in the deal.

These types of deals make a lot of money for three people. How can it be three people if there are only two people in a joint venture? I will explain this in a minute. First, let's discuss the two people who are obvious. The operator of the web site geared toward people who want cleaner teeth and the person who has the toothpaste. It does not necessarily have to be the manufacturer of toothpaste but could be someone who came across a closeout sale on the product. Let's say that you were shopping online and found someone who had 20, 000 toothpaste tubes of a special type that was manufactured in Switzerland which stopped selling over there and someone brought it to the United States. Now you can buy that product for 5 cents each. Believe me, there are plenty of those types of deals online and offline.

Now you have 20, 000 tubes of toothpaste that cost 5 cents each for a total cost of $1, 000.00. You contact the owner of the web site who markets to people with this special need, you offer a joint venture, wanting to sell the toothpaste as a package of five tubes for $19.95, and we will split the actual proceeds 50:50. Remember, you want to split the actual proceeds and not the actual profit because people are going to become very suspicious of what your actual costs were and what your actual profit is. You do not want to tell someone that your actual cost on the toothpaste was $1.50 because people understand how you bought it and are experienced when approached with joint ventures. Meaning, they could just call someone else and ask him or her the actual cost of this tooth-paste and what price that you likely paid for it? The best joint venture deals occur that when you assure them even when you have to split the proceeds 50:50 that even after the cost of you purchasing the merchandise, you can still make money even after the cost of you delivering the service. Remember, the other party also has an expense—it costs money to put together the e-mail list. You may spend thousands of dollars soliciting all of those leads. You want to set up the joint ven-ture and the person agrees to send out the e-mail five times. Every time that he sends out the e-mail he is sending it to 50,000 people, we only have 200 people responding, and if they purchase, the product sells for $19.95. This is a little under $4, 000 so $4, 000.00 for the spot is $20, 000. You split this two ways and each party receives $10, 000.00. Even though you might not have sold all of the toothpaste that you purchased, but your entire cost of the toothpaste was $1, 000.00 and your share of this joint venture was $10, 000.00 giving you a profit of $9, 000.00 and you still have plenty of toothpaste to sell. Even if the toothpaste had cost you $5,000.00 you are still sitting on a $5,000.00 profit and you could find another joint venture or continue this same joint venture later on to sell more toothpaste.

The third party that I mentioned before is the person who arranges this joint venture. There are people who develop a successful online income by connecting different parties who form these joint ventures meaning someone whom you may have developed a contact with such as other people who buy closeouts and sell closeouts. You could make that connection as a closeout broker. The way that you do this online with joint ventures is to search for different parties that offer prod-ucts or services that are either complimentary to each other or by using the resources of another party, can make money by selling the products or services.

One of the most successful joint venture agents that I have read about makes over

$200, 000.00 a month by specifically connecting different parties who have products that can be sold when they use each other's resources in a combined fashion. This online agent might find an individual who owns music tapes and the finds another web site that receives large traffic of people who are interested in the type of music that is on the tapes. On the other hand, he may find a tax attor-ney who is looking for clients and then offline source or e-mail broker that adver-tises towards the type of clients that the tax attorney would like to have. The advantage of doing all of this online is that it is easier to find joint venture oppor-tunities of people and services that you are interested in or to whom you can sell and it is also easier to find sources through the traffic that you would like to bring.

In other words, if you decide to focus on joint ventures in the clothing area then you could look online for plenty of sources of people who manufacture wholesale or retail clothing. You could find plenty of sources of traffic of people who are interested in that type of clothing. They could be wholesalers, manufacturers, distributors, closeout marketers, liquidators, retailers, flea market vendors or e-bay sellers. You can connect people online and even though you would think that everyone else has the same access to joint ventures that you do, you would be surprised at how many people overlook opportunities that are available online simply because they do not know where to look.

In my closeout business, I may have a closeout that is difficult to sell and I will be the first one to admit that it happens more often than I would like it to happen. I then look for closeout brokers who already have an existing e-mail list of 2,000 or 3,000 people who are serious closeout buyers. These 2,000 or 3,000 thousand people are people that I know are actively looking to buy closeouts. I then send out my closeout offering to his e-mail list and we split the proceeds as we have discussed. If the person who will be marketing your products or the person whom you are joining in the joint ventures with, if they are very familiar with the product that you are selling, then they will usually know your cost estimate.

There are specific times when you do not have to enter into a 50/50 venture. I still strongly recommend, especially when it is your first time arranging a joint venture between two parties who do not know each other, or you are forming a joint venture between yourself and another party whom you have not dealt with in the past, you should specifically hold yourself to a 50:50 deal. At the same time, make sure you do not give more than 50% of your share aware since you are entitled to that share because you are bringing assets into the equation that the other party does not have. Regardless of what that party says to you in the negotiations keep in mind, if they did not need you they would simply not be interested in the joint venture or they would not spend the time discussing it with you. If you see from the beginning that they are interested in the joint venture then you do not have to give them more than 50%. This 50% is what people expect and they already have an interest in doing business with you and therefore realize that you have something to bring to the table that can benefit them by marketing.

The same is true if you have developed an e-mail list of 50 to 100 thousand people, you could set up a joint venture with people who sell books, music tapes, DVD's, clothing or any items or services because now you have a source of traffic or potential clients that they can benefit from. In addition, if you have a web site that has a small amount of traffic or high amount of traffic, as long as your web site is geared towards a very specific market place, you have a very strong asset to offer to a potential joint venture partners. If you have a web site that caters to house painters, then you find someone who has clothing for sale that is geared to house painters then you can contact the owner of the clothing, the manufacturer or even a retailer of the clothing and let them know that you receive 1, 000 visitors from house painters ever month. Those visitors to your web site are very valuable to them since your traffic is specifically their target audience the conversion ratio may be a lot higher than 1%, the conversion ratio could be even as high as 20%. Therefore, you have something of value to offer to them even the traffic that your site has or the number of e-mails on your list is very low, as long as it is directly targeted you will be able to offer something of significant value to the other party. Now I am sure that you will be tempted to ask for more than 50% because let's say for example you do not have 1,000 names on your e-mail list but you have 10,000. Then you are offering something of extreme benefit to the other party. I would still suggest that you stick to the 50:50 rule because anytime that you take advantage of someone that person will remember. Since everything in life consists of networks and circles of people, what you do in relation to one person will eventually be known by other people. You do not know in what direction the circle turns and when you will want a joint venture with an associate of that person or that business working in that circle. You will want to have them as a reference in order to enter a new joint venture. At the same time, it always pays to keep other people's interests in mind because if you enter into a win-win situation then you will be insured of continued good will which help you produce long-term business which is what every online business needs.

If you are forming joint ventures as an agent, meaning that you are looking for different parties to connect and sometimes those joint ventures can consist of three or more parties and each party receives an equal percentage of the proceeds of each sale. The way that you are compensated is by taking a certain percentage from the sales off the top, meaning that most joint venture agents take roughly 7% as a fee of the gross proceeds. The rest of the proceeds are split 50/50 by the joint venture partners. When you are arranging this joint venture and after your research is done, you present your findings to both of the parties and you expect that this deal will produce $20,000.00 in sales then your fee would be $1,400.00.

If you have success in bringing together joint venture partners and your services are in demand or you develop a good reputation and people approach you to find joint venture partners for them. You could do either of the following things. You could charge up front for your consulting services, meaning your work in finding a joint venture partner for them. You could charge a higher percentage of the fee. You can charge a minimum compensation fee, which means that regardless of the actual proceeds that come from the sales, you are entitled to at least the first $1, 000.00 for your efforts.

The reason why businesses and individuals will agree to this is that they that realize without your effort they would not have the business resulting from that joint venture. In this case, they are willing to take a chance giving up a small profit on the deal even if it is the only profit from the deal because at the same time, they want the chance to benefit for the possible profit from the deal. In this type of situation if you enter a joint venture between two parties and one party has an e-mail list of 10,000 names and the list is geared towards investors who enjoy reading investment publications that deal with small caps. Then you locate an author of a small cap book. You would approach the author and explain that you know someone who has a tremendous interest in your book and he has an e-mail list that goes out on a weekly list dealing with important investment issues that effect small cap arena and the list always features a new book which is of interest to readers. Further, the readers of the e-mail list have grown accustomed to respecting the books that are featured and recommended in the newsletter. The author of that small cap book will be very interested because now he can potentially reach up to 10, 000 people as customers for his book. When you approach the owner of the e-mail list you let him know that you found another product that he can sell through the newsletter, which is going out regardless every week, and he has an option to bring in more revenue from his e-mails by featuring this book. In this situation, you bring both parties together but before you introduce them to one another, you make them sign an agreement that they cannot go behind your back and have to make a commitment agreement through you.

Now, they may be concerned that they may eventually find each other on their own, so therefore you make part of the agreement read that for a one year period from the time that you introduce them they cannot make a deal without you and all of this negotiated. As long as both parties are acting in good faith, then they should respect the services you are providing and their intention will not be to go behind your back because they know that if the joint venture is successful that you introduce them to other joint ventures, which will mean more profit.

Now you bring both of these parties together with the agreement intact and tell the owner of the e-mail newsletter that if he sells the book to 200 people out of his 10,000 readers, that he will receive $10.00 per book which will equal $2,000.00. If he does this 4 times over the course of two months, then it will be another potential $8, 000.00 for the owner of the e-mail newsletter. The author of the book may spend $3.00 a book to print it. If he is receiving $10.00 a book, he will have a $7.00 profit, but if he were receiving the proceeds of 800 times the $7.00, it would equal $5, 600.00. This would be income that the book author did not have before selling his book.

As the agent who arranges this deal, you should take a certain percentage. If you are concerned that the author and the owner of the e-mail list do not want to spend any money out of pocket because they are not big business people and have limited resources, then you want to set up the deal so that you are only making money off the sale proceeds. Since you are only making money off the sale proceeds you do not have any other sources of income related to this deal you would be rightly entitled to a higher percentage of the deal. You have the choice to ask for 10% of the proceeds off the top of the deal and everything else is split 50:50. If they sell 800 books total and each book, retails for $20.00 you will earn $1, 600.00 from $16, 000.00 and the other two parties each share the rest. Even though this now means that the share of the author is now smaller he should still be excited about this deal even if he is making a smaller amount of money because otherwise he would have made no money on the deal if you had not brought the deal together. This is still an extra $6.00 times $800.00 or $4, 800.00 that the author receives. The same is true for the owner of the e-mail newsletter. $800.00 times $10.00 equals $10, 000.00 so now instead of receiving $8, 000.00 he will receive $7, 200.00 and he may actually receive less since your own 10% comes off the top of the $16, 000.00 so you have $14, 600.00 left and he is receiving 50% of that. Both the owner of the e-mail newsletter and the author of the book both gain from the deal because this is money that is being produced by a joint venture deal that they did not initiate or create.

Therefore, you can see that arranging these deals online can be very lucrative. You can actually set up an online business that is specifically aimed at bringing different partners together and forming joint ventures that will produce different sources of revenue for all parties involved.

Chapter Twenty-Four

You should set up an affiliate program for your site. An affiliate program is one in which other web site owners and owners of e-zines and anyone can sign up to sell your products and services. The way that this happens is that in conventional affiliate program people will feature your product or service on their site by having an ad or a link that will take visitors to your site. The owner of a site that deals in raising pets will have an affiliate program where he will reward owners of other websites for bringing visitors to his or her sites. If the owner of the pet raising web site sells pet food, he can have an affiliate program that pays 10% commission of sales that originated by outside sites. If someone has a site that also is geared towards people who want to know how to raise their pets properly then they could have a link for the primary site and any visitor who clicks on the link is taken to the primary site. If they make a purchase on that web site, the owner of the site who sent the visitor receives a commission for sending the visitor.

So, here we have site A. Site A is the organizer of the affiliate program. Let's call site A

"Good Pets.com". Site A sells all types of pet products including pet food. Site B will be called

"Healthy Pets.com". Site B joins the affiliate program of Site A. Every time site B sends visitors to site A they will be compensated for any sales that are produced by the visitors that they send. Therefore, site A benefits because they receive more traffic and more customers than they would have otherwise. They spend less money on advertising because there is someone else who is spending money on advertising and bringing customers to their site and they have an overall increase of sales. Also what happens is that if you have a site that is devoted to healthy pets and you are currently spending $1, 000.00 per month on advertising and you are able to bring in 10, 000 visitors, then you are paying 50 cents per visitor. Using the 1% conversion ratio, it is costing you $10.00 to bring in 100 visitors who will give you a certain amount of profit. Another hint, if you have 100 sites and each site is sending you 100 visitors that is free traffic besides the commission that the site receives. Your conversion ratio is actually not important in this situation because the only thing that is important is what you can afford to give those other sites as a commission that is high enough to attract them to join your affiliate program and to send customers to your site.

In other words, if you have 100 sites that have joined your affiliate program and each one of the sends you visitors, that traffic is free since you do not have to pay for the site. If you have other websites who are already sending you some of their traffic or are either advertising or have a following of people who visit their sites and may click on your links and will be taken to your site. Remember, you did not have to spend any money at all to bring in those visitors to your site and now if out of a $100.00 sale you give a $10.00 or $20.00 commission, you still keep $80.00.

For example, if you sell a $100.00 item which gives you a $50.00 profit. Consider advertising and your conversion ratio, your cost for that $50.00 profit may be as high as $30.00. If you use an affiliate program, you might only have to give $5.00 or $10.00 of your profit away as a commission for people who bring in sales to your site or lead people to the site. The way that this works is that there is software that allows you to track where your visitors came from and automatically updates the owners of the websites or e-zines who send you traffic. You will then know that they are receiving something for the traffic they are sending you and they know that you have a meticulous system that keeps track of all the traffic that you are receiving. On the other hand, you will also benefit because you know who to send out the checks to, which affiliates are the best affiliates and you can reward those people to get them to increase the methods that they are using to send you traffic. Hopefully, this way you will receive more traffic.

There are many websites that cater just to this market such as "commissionjunction .com" that allow people for a fee to set up an affiliate program on their site and keep track of your affiliate program and will send out payments to your affiliates. As you can see, there is an entire infrastructure available to help you properly set up this type of program.

On this note, if your site is catering to a very specific market you should also consider joining affiliate programs that have a product or service that directed towards your market.

If you have a book devoted towards managing a restaurant, you sell this book from your web site, and you are tracking a lot of traffic from people who are interested in opening up their own restaurant you already know your traffic. Now you need to look for affiliate programs that sell products or services to this market. You may find software programs sold at a site that is specifically aimed towards people who run restaurants. You could place a link for that software on your site and therefore, every time you send a visitor to that site, you will receive a commission from the sale. The reason why you can expect to have a higher response rate is because the visitors that you are receiving to your site are interested in running their restaurants better and therefore they will respond to any offerings that will help them run their restaurants better.

How do you make an affiliate program work? Well, you either you offer an affiliate program with a high commission or you join an affiliate program with a high commission. The most important part besides insuring that the person who runs the affiliate program is reliable and honest, is making sure that the product you are offering, whether you have an affiliate program and your affiliates are taking your links and putting them on your site or if you are joining an affiliate program and putting someone else's links on your site, you must make sure that the traffic or target market is closely connected to the product or service that your are offering. If they are mutually compatible, meaning that there is products or services that fit then you will be able to make plenty of money.

One of the best ways to insure that your affiliates join your affiliate program and keep promoting your product is by constantly offering them tools that will enable them to sell successfully whatever you are offering. You could design banner ads for them, write articles that they can send up to their customers or e-mail lists which would take away a lot of the work that they would otherwise have to do themselves. This way if you write the articles, you design them, they only have to send them out to customers, they only have to post the articles on the web site, and they merely have to follow the campaigning that you have already outlined. If you join an affiliate program with another web site and want to insure that you are able to send traffic to that affiliate site then what you want to do is not just put a link on their site, but you need to make sure the link is related and also you want to give people a reason to click on the link.

I have seen websites that have made plenty of money just by having links to other people's affiliate programs. How did they make their money? They attract a large amount of traffic to their sites. They have a theme to their sites and develop a following. Then they feature the different products or services on their site and provide clickable links to read more about their products or services. The customers then go to other sites and if they are still interested in what is being offered they make a purchase. The chances are that they will make a purchase since those sites are specifically created to sell different affiliate programs or affiliated products or services are geared specifically towards their interests.

In other words, if you are careful to create a site that caters to baseball cards and customers visit your site because of your articles or what you offering then you should have links on your site that go to other sites that have products or services specifically aimed to baseball card collectors. This could be baseball shirts, collectibles, and figurines and of course cards. When you consider all of the different affiliate programs you can join, make sure to join the ones with the highest commission. When you join the ones that give you the highest commission, I do not just mean the highest commission per se, because you could figure that out on your own. You do not need to read any book to discover this. You want to see what the actual conversion ratio is of people who followed that affiliate link. When you go to a web site find out what their conversion ratio is on their site. If there are two site that sell baseball cards and one site offers a 10% commission and another site offers 20% commission, but the site who offers 10% closes three times as many sales then you would rather send your visitors to the site that has the 10% commission and closes more sales. You would be receiving a 30% commission as opposed to a 20% commission. The key is in determining what the closing ratios of the sites are where you are sending your traffic. When joining an affiliate program make sure that the manager has a high closing ratio or at least has a higher closing ratio than its competitors have. This is a good way to choose what type of affiliate program to join. Most affiliate program managers such as "commissionjunction.com" or "linkshare.com" show you and tell what actual conversion ratios actually are for different banner ads. You need to use the links and banners that will produce the best results and you need to join sites with the highest closing ratio.

How do you get people to actually click on your links? You need to write interesting articles and around the article have links to the products or services that you are promoting. Alternatively, at the end of the article you have links where people can now check out the items that you have for sale. Meaning, I personally enjoy reading books on investing. If I go to a web site that has a great article on an investment book, I will more than likely to click on the link if it is part of the article that is discussing a certain type of investment approach. If that approach is further described in the book and I have read the article in which that book is quoted two or three times, then I will be interested in clicking on the link to read more about the book. When I arrive at the site and use the site to buy the book, then the owner of the site who sent me there will receive a commission. If I specifically arrive to a site and only see a site full of links for investment books, then I have no motivation to click on any of the links because I am not sure if any of those books will actually benefit me. If there is something there to give me a reason to click on one of the links and explains to me why I would want to click on the links, then I would be more likely to do it. This is the way to have a successful affiliate program from both ends as an affiliate or as an affiliate program manager.

Chapter Twenty-Five

One of the most lucrative opportunities to make money online today is through eBay. The reason that I say today, is because I literally mean that eBay allows you to make money within the same day that you start using it. eBay, as most of us know, is an online marketplace that acts as an auction house that allows individuals, whether they are private sellers or businesses, to put up auctions on the site. These auctions can range anywhere in length from one day to as much as 30 days for real estate auctions. The reason why eBay is so promising is because there are currently over 20 million registered users on the site. In other words, you have the opportunity to place an auction in front of as many as 20 million users. Not only that but you also have the opportunity to make connections, build long term customer relationships, and develop sales leads. Think about how much easier it is to put your slow moving merchandise on eBay as opposed to hosting a weeklong sale in your store, or what about putting up your items for sale instead of having to spend an entire weekend at a flea market? Remember, in addition to being able to put your merchandise up for sale on eBay, you can also contact other eBay sellers and wholesale merchandise to them that they need in order to have what to put up for auction.

eBay is definitely one of the surest ways to start making immediate income online. I know of certain businesses that use eBay to sell as much as $5,000 worth of merchandise a week! How many stores do you know that have that type of sales volume. And the best part about eBay is that as I mentioned earlier, once you have a customer you can continue to sell to that customer even after the auction has ended. If you want to read more about the actual details of starting an eBay business, or on how to take your business on to eBay, you should read "The Truth about eBay" and "Secrets of eBay".

I have actually developed a business where I supply merchandise for eBay sellers. The reason why the business has been able to help eBay sellers make a decent amount of money is because I offer brand name closeouts that are available way below the original wholesale cost. My site, www.closeoutexplosion.com is actually based on the information that you have been reading in this book. How is that for proof that this book can really help you?

Conclusion

Now you have arrived at the most important part of this book. This is the part of the book that will instruct you to review everything that you have learned. You should review the notes that you have been making, to think about all of the ideas that came to you as you were reading the book. Now you need to take everything that you have learned, combine it, form a business plan as discussed and then you need start implementing the plans that you have formulated. Without action, thought is worthless. What is important in business life is the actual end results produced. End results are only produced when action is taken.

You now have a tremendous opportunity to develop for yourself either a part time income, a full time income or just to make some money on the side when you need it or maybe just to develop yourself an extra source of money for a vacation, buy a high priced item or just have some extra spending money. You could donate to charity or give it to your children or grandchildren. The most important thing to remember is that unless you take action and actually take what you have learned and utilize it you will not be able to benefit. Oh the other hand, if you are a successful minded person, people with positive attitude and are willing to try new ideas, if you do have the energy and motivation to start a new online venture and actually put your new knowledge into action, then you will have a very good change of being successful online.

Remember, it is always important to focus on the positives in life. Do not look at how many people have failed online because those people did not have the same information that you have available today. They did not have the same resources or tools that are widely available online for you to use. They did not have access to web designers the way that you do. They did not have access at the cost that you do. They did not have access to the level of advertising and the price of advertising that you do. They did not have access to the products or services that you do. Therefore, you have a lot in your favor and not only that, you can remember as discussed in this book you can study the competition and study other people who are successful and people who have failed. Basically, instead of now having to experiment with your business through trial and error, you can learn from people who already succeeded in the online market that you want to join. Instead of having to be the pioneer as most of the first online entrepreneurs had to be, you can now can be a veteran, work on the backs of other people's undertakings and prior work, and learn from the lessons of their work. You can develop a successful online business using the knowledge and information that has already been produced by countless entrepreneurs who were not able to succeed online.

With this thought, I urge you to continue to study, learn, and amass information. Once again, you are more than welcome to contact me if you have any questions, need any advice, or simply have any comments on this book.

Thank you very much and I hope that you have enjoyed the book.

If you are ready to start your own online business and are looking for products to sell make sure to visit www.closeoutexplosion.com

To receive more ideas on taking your business online, including personal consulting from the author visit www.DonnyLowy.com

About the Author

Donny Lowy is a recognized and well-respected entrepreneur who has started and operated many successful online businesses.

As an online entrepreneur he is sought after for his valuable consulting services which have helped many individuals and businesses take advantage of the lucrative opportunities found online.

0-595-30958-5

Printed in the United States
24801LVS00003B/402

9 780595 309580